Media Representation of Migrant Workers in China

Linguistic Insights

Studies in Language and Communication

Edited by Maurizio Gotti,
University of Bergamo

Volume 177

PETER LANG
Bern · Bruxelles · Frankfurt am Main · New York · Oxford · Warszawa · Wien

Wei Wang

Media Representation of Migrant Workers in China

Identities and Stances

PETER LANG
Bern · Bruxelles · Frankfurt am Main · New York · Oxford · Warszawa · Wien

Bibliographic information published by die Deutsche Nationalbibliothek
Die Deutsche Nationalbibliothek lists this publication in the Deutsche Nationalbibliografie; detailed bibliographic data is available on the Internet at ‹http://dnb.d-nb.de›.

British Library Cataloguing-in-Publication Data: A catalogue record for this book is available from The British Library, Great Britain.

Library of Congress Control Number: 2017954814

ISSN 1424-8689 hb.
ISBN 978-3-0343-1436-7 pb.
ISBN 978-3-0343-3202-6 MOBI
ISSN 2235-6371 eBook
ISBN 978-3-0351-0588-9 eBook
ISBN 978-3-0343-3201-9 EPUB

This publication has been peer reviewed.

Wabernstrasse 40, CH-3007 Bern, Switzerland
info@peterlang.com, www.peterlang.com

Contents

Preface

The unprecedented economic development and rapid urbanisation in China over the past four decades has propelled massive internal migration. Large numbers of the population have migrated from the countryside to towns and cities, especially to megalopolises such as Beijing, Shanghai and Guangzhou, usually individuals in search of jobs and higher wages. This large population has become the main labour force in China's recent massive economic boom. Official statistics from China's National Bureau of Statistics (2016) place the number of internal migrants in China at about 20% of its population of 1.37 billion, having increased from roughly 30 million in 1989 to more than 277.47 million in 2015. Yet when migrants leave their homesteads, they tend to suffer from many difficulties, such as identity crisis and social injustice, and, further, the existing social system has to meet the challenges of resettling this population into a normative urban life. These issues and problems are perpetuated by China's longstanding social structure and political system. While this social phenomenon has drawn the attention of researchers from a wide range of socio-political studies including sociology, economics, anthropology, and political studies, this book sets out to investigate how the public media in China represent this distinctive social group. This book will provide a sociolinguistic analysis of how identities of, and stances towards, migrant workers have been represented in China's public media, such as print media, web pages, and TV programs, and how these representations have been constructed by the media.

Drawing on discourse analysis and sociolinguistic theories, this book explores how their identities and the stances taken towards them have been constructed, transformed, and mediated in China's media in response to the rapid social change in China. The theories underpinning this socio-oriented discourse study include (critical) discourse analysis (Fairclough 1993, 1995, 2015; Blommaert 2005; van Dijk 1988, 2011), sociocultural linguistic theories on identity (Bucholtz and Hall 2004, 2005, 2008; Bucholtz 1999, 2002), discourse and identity research

(Benwell and Stokoe 2006; Daiute and Lightfoot 2004; De Fina and Georgakopoulou 2012), stance-taking theories (Bois 2007; Jaffe 2009), and many more, which together provide the researcher with a repertoire of tools for conceptualising, analysing and interpreting the data.

For the analysis of identity as constituted in linguistic interaction, sociocultural linguistic researchers on identity hold that identity is the product rather than the source of linguistic and other semiotic practices (e.g. Blommaert 2005; Bucholtz and Hall 2005). They claim that identity is fundamentally a social and cultural phenomenon that emerges from linguistic and other semiotic practices. Identity in this research tradition is not simply viewed as a psychological mechanism of self-classification that is reflected in people's social behaviour but rather as something that is constituted through social action, and especially through language (Bucholtz and Hall 2005: 588). In narrative identity research, narrative is considered as the 'basic', most 'essential', mode of human communication that can index identity. Narrative is also regarded as experience-as-told and as made social (Blommaert 2005:84). In other words, it is regarded as a basic human way of making sense of the world as we lead 'storied lives' (Riessman 1993). In this sense, narrative is constitutive of reality as well as of identity and subjectivity.

Stance, as defined by Bois (2007), is a public act by a social actor, achieved interactively with others through language, gesture, and other symbolic forms. By using these explicit communication means, social actors "simultaneously evaluate objects, position subjects (themselves and others), and align with other subjects, with respect to any salient dimension of the sociocultural field" (Bois 2007:163). From linguistic or sociolinguistic perspectives, there are various terms that have been used to describe different types of stance-taking, such as footing, alignment, positioning, and addressivity (see Jaffe 2009 for a detailed summary). Bois (2007:139) argues that stance is "one of the most important things we do with words," and it is "a linguistically articulated form of social action".

Themes covered in the book include identities of and stances towards migrant workers constructed in public media, including newspapers, web pages, magazines and TV programs. It also explores the interactions between various media participants and the media practices and processes that construct these media products.

Objectives of the book are to

- explore interrelationship between media representation of migrant workers and social change in contemporary China;
- examine how identities of and stances towards migrant workers have been constructed, transformed and mediated in China's media discourse;
- investigate the media strategies and practices constructing these media products.

This book aims at providing a conceptual advance in understanding one of the most noteworthy components of the Chinese population against a backdrop of high mobility in China. It also provides a comprehensive study of how the media representation of migrant workers is interacting with the sociocultural transformation in China. The findings and discussions of the book offer critical insights into media discourse and practice in contemporary China which will be of interest to scholars and research students in discourse studies, sociolinguistics, media and communication studies, and China studies.

Acknowledgements

This book is based on my research conducted on Chinese media discourse between 2010 to the present. I am grateful to the publishers below for granting me permission to reproduce the following articles: Taylor and Francis Group (London: www.tandfonline.com) for my article "Coffee and 18 years of endeavour: stances towards white-collar migrants in China", published in *Journal of Multicultural Discourses* (2014) 9(2), 134–148, which forms the basis for Chapter 4 "White-collar migrant workers in public media"; John Benjamins Publishing Company for my article "Co-construction of migrant workers' identities on a TV talk show in China", published in Tsung and Wang (ed.) *Contemporary Chinese Discourse and Social Practice in China* (2015), 125–142, (Amsterdam/Philadelphia: https://www.benjamins.com/catalog/scld.4), which forms the basis for Chapter 5 "Construction of migrant workers' identities on a TV talk show".

My sincere thanks go to colleagues at the University of Sydney for their encouragement and support during the writing of this book: Yingjie Guo, Linda Tsung, Bonnie McDougall, Brian Paltridge, Yixu Lu, and Irene An. I also thank anonymous reviewers of the original journal articles and the present book chapters who have made constructive suggestions.

Also, I am indebted to the China Studies Centre at the University of Sydney for providing me with adequate funding to attend the *International Conference on Language, Power and Identity in Asia* (Leiden, the Netherlands in 2016), during which I presented part of the findings in this book and received productive comments and suggestions.

My special thanks go to Tigger Wise who has proofread the whole manuscript with her careful attention to details. I would also like to thank Lian Liu and Liang Xia for their meticulous help with the data analysis for Chapter 3 and preparation of appendix.

My special thanks also go to my friends and colleagues in China who have provided assistance with the data collection and, especially, the access to the media. Without their help, it would not have been possible to complete this project.

I am also extremely grateful for the editorial guidance provided by Laura Diegel and Adrian Stähli at the Peter Lang Publishing Group.

Finally, but most of all, my thanks go to my wife Dan and lovely son Jeff, whose love and inspiration have meant so much to me.

1. Migrant workers and public media in China

1.1. Internal migrant workers in China

Along with the substantial economic development in China, the recent 40 years have witnessed a massive internal migration in China from rural to urban, from west to east, and from the less developed to the developed areas. It has been a spectacular socio-economic phenomenon in China's history. According to the National Bureau of Statistics of China (2016), the total of migrant workers reached 277.47million in 2015 among its total population of 1.37 billion. Migrant workers employed in the cities take up 70% of a total of 382.4 million urban employments. That simply means that more than 20 % of the total population in China are on the move now, not residing in the place where they were born and are registered for their *hukou* (Chinese: 户口, i.e. the household registration system). Most migrants in this historical period are from the western or less developed areas, migrating to the cities or more developed regions in the eastern coastal areas, especially the megacities like Beijing, Shanghai, Guangzhou, and Shenzhen. Even though population migration is an integral part of urbanisation and modernization, this massive mobility in China has given rise to enormous social changes in China. Despite the significant contribution of this social group to providing a labour force for China's economy, it has presented unprecedented challenges to the existing social system. One example is that while leaving home at a premium age, many migrant workers have left their children back home, resulting in millions of young children living without proper support and care from their parents. That leads to serious social problems in the rural areas. In addition, for those children coming along with their parents to big cities, without local *hukou*, their attendance at proper schools in the cities becomes a big issue for the local city governments.

The social problems brought about by the massive migration much stem from the binary *hukou* system (i.e. agricultural vs. non-agricultural) that has existed in China for over half a century from 1958 to 2015. A *hukou* is a record in the system of household registration required by law in mainland China. A household registration record officially identifies a person as a resident of an area and includes identifying information such as name, parents, spouse, date of birth, and even work place (Chinese: 工作单位). A *hukou* is also a family register in many contexts since the household registration record is issued per family, and usually includes the births, deaths, marriages, divorces, work places, and moves, of all members in the family. From 1958 to 2015, the household registration was broadly categorised to 'agricultural' (rural) and 'non-agricultural' (urban) types. As an instrument of the planned economy, *hukou* limited mass migration from the land to the cities to ensure some structural stability. For some time, the Chinese Ministry of Public Security continued to justify the *hukou* system not only on public order grounds, and also that it provided demographic data for government central planning. Indeed, the *hukou* system has been justified by some scholars as increasing the stability of China. However, against the background of the current high mobility of the population and social change in China, the binary *hukou* system has come under heavy criticism and has been regarded as deeply hindering the necessary social mobility in the society. On July 30, 2014, the State Council of China promulgated a decree on "Further reform of the household registration system", and explicitly called for the establishment of a unified *hukou* system (State Council of China 2014a). It was announced that the demarcation of the agricultural and non-agricultural *hukou* should be eradicated and a unified registration system for residents be adopted. This indicates that over half a century of "agriculture" and "non-agricultural" binary household registration has faded from history. The move will deeply transform the social order with the anticipation that the social gap between the urban and rural will be narrowed from now on.

The vast majority of China's migrant workers are farmers from the country's interior and western provinces who were inspired to leave their home villages due to a series of factors, such as, employment opportunities in cities, attractions associated with urban life, and freedom from family obligations. Since the advent of China's 'Reform and Opening' in 1979, the first wave of migration started from the early 1980s with people from inland areas seeking employment in major cities and special economic zones located in the south and east of the country. Along with the 'Develop the West' (Chinese: 西部大开发) campaigns in the 21st century, many inland cities such as Chongqing and Xi'an have also become attractive destinations for those migrant workers who might like to choose places closer to home. Recent statistics reports from China National Bureau of Statistics (2016) also indicate that more migrant workers now choose to move to cities in their home provinces rather than those in other provinces.

As an integral component of Chinese development, this floating population has been providing cheap labour for the Chinese economy. Migrant workers take up the majority of the work force in the manufacturing industry, producing daily utilities and products all across the country. They are also the main workforce in construction sites for buildings, roads, bridges, and other major infrastructures. Also, the migrant workers are the main workforce in the family care sector to take care of others' elders and young children while leaving their own at home unattended. This floating population has made tremendous contributions to the economic development of the recent 40 years.

However, as noticed by many scholars in social sciences (e.g. Fan 2008; Gaetano and Jacka 2004; Jacka 2005, 2006; Jacka et al. 2011, 2013; Wong et al. 2007; Xu, F. 2000; Yan 2008), migrant workers moving to cities are institutionally inferior and socially marginalised. They are far from welcomed by city governments and local urbanites, who usually attribute social problems to the arrival of these migrants. On an institutional level, migrant workers' rural or non-local *hukou* inhibits their access to the State provided or subsidised goods and services such as health care, housing, pensions, and education for their children. All these have limited their upward mobility in the society. In addition, on the social level, migrant workers face inherent discrimination by the established urban residency. Rather than integrating into the social networks of urbanites, migrant workers typically find themselves dwelling in an isolated component of society that consists of their fellow countrymen.

This social isolation further lends itself to discrimination and makes it easier for the urbanites to blame the new migrants as invaders and potential criminals who interfere with the established social orders in the cities. As Wang and Zuo (1999: 278) note, "the stereotype of rural migrants is that they are uneducated, ignorant, dirty, and also have high propensities to be criminals". In other words, all these have led to a discourse of abnormality around migrant workers in China (see more in Chapter 5).

Recent years have also witnessed a clear split in this floating population after years of hard work in cities. While a majority of the population might choose to migrate to cities permanently after working there for a long time, some of the population move back for marriage or a more stable life after working away from home for a period of time. However, for those who decide to establish their families in cities and purchase their own property with the hope of enjoying better social resources such as health care, education, and entertainment for themselves and their families, their settlement to cities would create more stresses on the overcrowded urban space and the already overstretched public resources.

This social phenomenon of massive internal migration in China has been extensively examined and investigated by scholars in the fields of economics, geography, sociology, political studies, social welfare, education, media studies, and other social sciences. While most of the research is on the social and policy level, scant research has been done from a sociolinguistic perspective to explore how the public media in China represent the migrant workers. It is hoped that investigating the complexities and hybridity of contemporary media discourse in representing this turbulent process of migration in response to the sociocultural change of contemporary China can provide some fresh insights into this social phenomenon.

Consequently, against such a background of massive internal migration in China, this book sets out to explore how the media discourse in China represents identities of this floating population and the stances taken by different social groups towards them. In addition, the specific characteristics of the Chinese media system and its practice in media production will also be investigated.

1.2. Public media in China

As a significant site for ideological construction, the media play a leading role in the representation of social reality. From the early years of the Chinese Communist Party (CCP) in 1930s, the party (hereafter referred to the CCP) has exercised great control and influence on the public media. Since the founding of the People's Republic of China in 1949 and until the 1980s, almost all media outlets in Mainland China were State/Party-run. Chinese media, especially the large presses in Beijing, such as *People's Daily*, Xinhua News Agency, CCTV (China Central Television), and CNR (China National Radio), serve as the party's mouthpieces in support of the government's agenda and policies, and are always the sources of news for other small news agencies. The public media in China are usually closely guided by the authoritarian press practice. The regulatory agencies, such as the CCP Central Committee Publicity Department (Chinese: 中共中央宣传部) and State Administration of Press, Publication, Radio, Film and Television (Chinese：国家新闻出版广电总局), set strict regulations on subjects considered taboo by the government, including but not limited to the legitimacy of the Communist Party, the government policies in special regions such as Tibet and Xinjiang, pornography, and the banned religious topics.

In China, there is a dual track administration system to regulate media management. On the one hand, under the CCP, there are the Publicity Departments at all levels of CCP committees (i.e. central, provincial, prefectural, city and county) to take charge of ideology-related work, as well as its information dissemination system. These departments at all levels also enforce media censorship and control in China. On the other hand, on the governmental side, there are administrative departments to regulate and monitor press, publication, radio, films and television. At the central government level under the State Council, that is the State Administration of Press, Publication, Radio, Film and Television. At the local government levels (i.e. provincial, prefectural, city and county), there are local press, publication, radio and television administrations with the same functions. This dual track administration system, with its possible overlapping functions, puts the public media in

China under close regulation and control by both the party and the government. While the party's publicity departments steer more towards political and ideological orientation, the government agencies take more regulative and operational responsibilities. If there are any discrepancies in policy making and operational issues, the decision made by the party's Publicity Departments prevails.

Despite heavy government monitoring, however, along with the massive economic development, the Mainland Chinese media have become an increasingly commercial market, with growing competition, diversified contents and increasing independence in management. These huge changes in the media industry in China over the past four decades have profoundly affected media practice and coverage. Here below are three aspects of changes that might be the keys to understanding the contemporary public media in China.

First, the marketization of media institutions has changed the structure of media presses and forced them to consider financial benefits, an aspect which might never have concerned the State-run presses previously. Before the 1980s, the media in China was under the complete control of the Communist Party's publicity system. Following the opening-up and reform policy of the 1980s, the media's role in China has softened from being purely a mouthpiece of the party-state to what has been characterised as Party Publicity Incorporation (Chen and Chan 1998). The term Party Publicity Incorporation comes from Schmitter's (1974) concept of "state corporatism", which was used to analyse the post-WWI capitalist countries. This term is employed by researchers (e.g. Chen and Chan 1998; Pan et al. 2001) to examine the relationship between the mass media and the party in modern China. As suggested by the term Party Publicity Incorporation, although the media in China remains tightly controlled, it has lost its former totalitarian characteristics (Pan et al. 2001). China now is marked by transition from a Communist authoritarian state with a planned economic setup to an authoritarian state with a market economy. Along with being a mouthpiece of the party, the commodified media system in China has accommodated a large amount of entertainment and commercial information, which to some extent has diluted the party's restriction on the media. It could be said that there is a tension between the party's control and the emerging ideological de-emphasis along with the development of the market economy. According to Zhao (1998, 2008, 2011), ideological de-emphasis in today's China is tolerated just to the extent that the media do not defy party authority or policy. Meanwhile, both party officials and media managers stress the importance of meeting "financial" (i.e. market) and "social" (i.e. party) goals (Pan et al. 2001). This suggests that in addition to being part of the party's publicity system, the media have become profit seekers that need to pursue their own financial interests. In other words, the public media in modern China have to take the responsibilities of being a government mouthpiece on the one hand, and on the other, they have to run as a business to cater for the needs of the ever-increasing market-oriented economy. Despite becoming livelier, the scope for fundamental change in China's mass media is limited by the media's long-standing role as a mouthpiece of the party and the consequent paternalistic top-down approach to presenting issues (Zhao 2008, 2011).

Second, the economic difficulties facing the media industry have affected both the quality and content of news making. The past twenty years have seen major audience losses in traditional areas, such as newspaper readership, radio listeners, and TV watchers. While the State-run party mouthpieces still enjoy some financial support from the governments, the majority of local and regional newspapers and television stations have to seek funding for survival. This change in funding sources and ownership of presses has inevitably led to their diversified positions in news coverage and representation of social issues. In addition, profit seeking has led to fierce competition between the presses and among peer journalists. Cost-cutting measures and improved management systems have resulted in an increased workload for journalists, who have been ambivalently positioned in a commercial context where they have to strike a balance between being politically correct and being attractive to audiences.

The large scale restructuring of the media institutions that occurred from late 1990s to early 2000s saw the traditional separate institutions merging together under the names of media groups. For example, many radio stations and TV stations at provincial and municipal levels merged together to run more broadcast channels. Different newspapers merged to form media groups that manage a large variety of newspapers, magazines and digital media sites. Even within the same media groups, a clear distinction can be found between official and commercial media outlets. For instance, the traditional Party-run mouthpiece *People's Daily* formed a big media group, which also ran a commercial tabloid-styled newspaper called *Beijing Times* (Chinese: 京华时报) based in Beijing. *Beijing Times* has now become independent as a separate newspaper (see more details in Chapter 3). Such restructuring of the media industry has brought about huge changes in coverage and their operational models.

Third, the internet and other interactive digital and social media such as recently emerging *Weibo* (Chinese:微博，i.e. microblogging) and *Weixin* (Chinese: 微信，i.e. *WeChat*) have transformed the structure of the mass media and caused a convergence of formerly separate branches or forms of media that are now interdependent, and which often operate in one single physical space. The process of media production has become a more collaborative and interactive process than ever before. As will be illustrated in the following chapters, journalists working with one form of media such as TV programs might draw on sources and information from other forms such as the internet or newspapers in preparation of their programs. Even within one media press, journalists tend to collaborate closely in producing news items or programs. Whether working in newspapers, TV programs, or internet websites, journalists are finding it more and more difficult to produce a news item as the sole author without relying on others' collaboration.

These new developments in the media industry have led to drastic changes in the ways of media production and various power relationships in Chinese society. A critical examination of the discourse concerning internal migration in China's public media will provide insights into how media representation contributes to the complex struggle over meanings and power in China.

1.3. Names of migrant workers in Chinese media

While a large amount of research has explored the social phenomenon of internal migration and its impact on Chinese society through the lens of social and economic developments, little has been done to explore how this social group has been represented in China's media discourse from a sociolinguistic perspective. Prior to my detailed examination of media discourse and media practice in order to fill this gap, I would like to explain how this floating population has been named in the Chinese language and media discourse with a view to illuminating the media representation of this social group.

Names are a valuable source of information which can indicate a person's (or a group's) identity and status in society. As the most meaningful lexicon in the vocabulary of any language, names are the social emblem attached to every individual giving indications of their sex, historical period of birth, ethnicity, nationality, or even expected disposition. Universal as the phenomenon is, every society has its own naming practices and its own implications of such names for the construction of identity for individuals. In the Chinese language, many terms have been used by the media to refer to these internal migration workers since their emergence in early 1980s. The most commonly used terms are *Nongmin Gong* (Chinese: 农民工), *Dagong Ren* (Chinese: 打工人), *Dagong Zai/Mei* (Chinese: 打工仔/妹), *Beipiao Zu* (Chinese: 北漂族), and more recently *Xin Gongren* (Chinese: 新工人) and *Xin Shimin* (Chinese: 新市民). These terms have been used in different social contexts to refer to diverse types of migrants. How the migrant workers have been named during these years can also partially reflect their tough experiences of integration into urban social life.

Since the early 1980s and the advent of "reform and opening", migrant workers have been called *Dagong Zai/Mei,* which literally means working girls/boys. Implicit in these terms is a strongly derogative stigmatization. These terms first were used in Guangdong with clear local flavours. *Nongmin Gong* was adopted in the late 1980s and is still widely used in many circumstances both official and private. It is more neutral than *Dagong Zai/Mei. Beipiao Zu* refers to the floating population, especially in Beijing, who are often well educated and involved in more white-collared or artistic careers. In the new century, the terms *Xin Gongren* (新工人) and *Xin Shimin* (新市民) are both advocated by the government with the hope of curbing the discriminations against the migrant workers.

Among these terms, *Nongmin Gong* (which literally means peasant workers) is the most commonly used one, being widely adopted in public communication and media discourse since the 1980s. This term highlights the inherent double-tier identity of this social group, i.e. peasant and worker. The hybrid identity given to the population, who are '*nongmin*' (peasants) working as '*gongren*' (workers) in cities, is largely a result of the binary *hukou* system in China. It is very difficult for people from the countryside to obtain a city *hukou*, with which social welfare, education, and other benefits are affiliated. So it is not simply a supercilious term that the city people choose to name this floating population, but its derivation is much rooted in the social system in China.

In recent years this term *Nongmin Gong* has been under severe criticism due to its contemptuous nature. While the old generation of *Nongmin Gong* went to cities for a better wage and good fortune, the current young generation of *Nongmin Gong* have different life expectations and dispositions, such as personal pursuit of development and freedom (Jacka 2005, 2006). Along with migrant workers becoming the mainstay of employment in urban areas and the main force in the creation of GDP (gross domestic product) in China, how to transform the migrant worker to a new citizen in cities has become the key to the transformation and development of the country in the new period.

In such a context, the term *Xin Shimin* (literally new city residents) was created to refer to this social group, with an attempt to integrate this migrant group into its urban counterparts. According to Baidu (2017a), '*Xin Shimin*' was first used in 2006 in Qingdao, Shandong Province by the local government in an effort to standardise the many terms used to refer to the floating population, such as '*Dagong Ren', 'Nongmin Gong'*, etc., which might bear possible contemptuous tones. In July 2014, Premier Li Keqiang advocated the adoption of the term *Xin Shimin* to refer to migrant workers in a State Council executive meeting (State Council of China 2014b). While acknowledging the social contribution made by this floating population, he requested cessation of treating migrant workers as second class citizens. It is not common in Chinese history for a government head to be engaged in the naming of a social group in society. His advocacy of a new name for this social group is also underpinned by changes of the government's policy concerning this floating population. Among them, the most important is the government's attempt to abolish the rural-urban dual *hukou* system, which has had or will have a huge impact on the migrant workers.

In the term '*Xin Shimin*', their identity as city residents has been confirmed, differing only from the existing city residents with the word '*xin*' (i.e. new). The use of the term 'new city residents' aims at eradicating any possible contempt of this floating population. However, unfortunately, Premier Li's advocacy of the use of the term *Xin Shimin* has not been unswervingly followed by the public media, even by the party's own mouthpiece *People's Daily* (see more details in Chapter 3).

From the initial '*Dagong Zai/Mei*' in the 1980s to the recent '*Xin Gongren/Shimin*' in the 2010s, the trajectory of the naming practices for this social group has sketchily demonstrated the tough journey that the migrant workers have experienced in their endeavours to integrate into the urban life in China.

In this book, the terms floating population and migrant workers, rather than '*Nongmin Gong*' and '*Xin Shimin*' are used to refer to the internal migrants in China, regardless of their education background and the place and space that they are working in. It aims to avoid the possible disdainful tones that both '*Nongmin Gong*' and '*Xin Shimin*' might bring along, but also the term floating population can indicate that this social group possesses strong unstable features of moving back and forth between urban/rural or developed/underdeveloped areas. Most of them work in cities all year around and only go back home for holidays, especially for the Spring Festival. This leads to the phenomenal Spring Travel Season (Chinese: 春运) in China when millions of people return home from work or study before the Spring Festival. Owing to the large number of interprovincial travellers, special arrangements are made by railways, buses and airlines starting from 15 days before the Chinese New Year's Day. It is regarded as the largest annual human migration in the world.

1.4. Overview of chapters

Along with the rise of internal migration in China since early 1980s, media coverage of migrant workers is abundant in all types of channels, print, broadcast, and social media. However, there are significant differences between how the migrant workers are represented in different media in mainland China.

This book features several chapters examining the media representation of migrant workers and the media practices used to construct, transform and mediate the identities of and stances towards this social group in China. Drawing on a sociolinguistic constructionism perspective, this book delineates these sociolinguistic construction processes in the light of recent socioeconomic changes in China.

Chapter 1 introduces the background of migrant workers in China, illustrates the key features in China's public media, and discusses how this social group of migrant workers has been named in the public media over the past 40 or so years in China.

Chapter 2 sets out the theoretical foundation of this book, reviewing four themes which are interrelated in addressing the research focuses under examination. The first theme involves the sociolinguistic theories that have been adopted to illuminate Chinese discourse analysis. This thread of review includes discussion of the traditional variationist sociolinguistic approach and the recent sociocultural linguistic approach. The second stream of review covers some foundational concepts drawn from critical discourse analysis, including text, genre, discourse, and discursive event, that underpin the media discourse analysis carried out in this book. The third thread is a review of previous literature on media discourse analysis and, in particular, media narrative. This section considers the concepts of genre and media narrative as a text type as well as a discursive activity or practice. The fourth thread reviews the literature on the sociolinguistic construction of identity and stance in media discourse. This thread considers how identity and stance have been constructed and mediated linguistically in media discourse.

Chapter 3 explores the media representation of Chinese internal migrant workers in the public media with a focus on six influential

Chinese newspapers, including *People's Daily, Jiefang Daily, Southern Daily, Beijing Times, Xinmin Evening News* and *Southern Metropolis Daily*. Of these, three are traditional party-run broadsheets and three are tabloid styled metropolitan papers, geographically representing newspapers from the major cities: Beijing, Shanghai and Guangzhou. Drawing on discourse analysis and sociolinguistic theories on identity and stance, this chapter illustrates how the migrant workers have been framed and represented in these newspapers in China with a view to revealing diverse socio-political viewpoints on and stances towards this distinctive social group.

Chapter 4 examines the circulation of two Chinese phrases *"he kafei"* (drinking coffee) and *18 nian fendou* (18 years of endeavour) concerning white collar migrant workers in Chinese media discourse. These two widespread phrases and the debate around them were initiated from a magazine article "I'm finally able to drink coffee together with you after 18 years of endeavour" （Chinese: 我奋斗了18年才和你坐在一起喝咖啡） (see Appendix II), originally published by *China Youth* (Issue 24, 2004), and republished by *Duzhe* (a leading general magazine in China) in 2005. In addition, drawing on a sociocultural linguistic perspective on identity (Bucholtz and Hall 2005) and stance-taking theories (Bois 2007; Jaffe 2009), this chapter examines how authors have constructed identities of and take stances towards white-collar migrants in China's media discourse. This chapter will analyse the linguistic manifestations of taking divergent stances in both the print and Internet media in China. These differentiated stances can be argued as specific instances of what Hodge and Kress (1993) refer to as the production of social difference in texts.

Chapter 5 investigates the media practice in transforming the *Nongmin Gong*'s personal life experiences into media discourse. Drawing on sociolinguistic theories and ethnographic field work, this chapter examines how the TV crews co-construct and represent the identities of migrant workers (i.e. *Nongmin Gong*) on a TV talk show program in China, called *"China's Nongmin Gong"* (Chinese: 中国农民工), which was launched by Guizhou Satellite TV (GZSTV) in China in 2007. This chapter finds that the TV crews, in order to fulfil the specific social objective of the TV program, adopt various discursive practices to represent the migrant workers' identities.

Chapter 6 draws the empirical studies together and discusses how these analyses of the public media representation and practices in China can contribute to our understandings of the media discourse of migrant workers in light of the social and cultural change in China. This chapter discusses the media representation, interaction, and production around the coverage of migrant workers in China and considers how the identities and stances have been constituted and mediated in Chinese media discourse. This chapter concludes with suggestions for future directions of media discourse analysis in Chinese contexts.

2. Media discourse analysis from a sociolinguistic perspective

To analyse media discourse, we cannot avoid starting with discussing the concept of representation, which occupies a pivotal position in cultural and media studies. Briefly, representation refers to the production of meaning through language or any signifying system (Hall 2013). In this sense, we can use language to represent anything, such as people or event, in either the 'real' world of real objects or imaginary worlds of fictional objects. As a social practice, representation is ubiquitous and permeates into any process of our expression through language. As Hall (2013:1) argues, "Representation is an essential part of the process by which meaning is produced and exchanged between members of a culture". It connects meaning and language to culture. To represent something in language means using language to say something meaningfully to other people (Hall 2013). In the same vein, media representation concerns the way in which the media portray particular individuals, social groups, communities, experiences, ideas, events, or topics from a particular ideological or value perspective.

As Hall (2013) illustrates, there are three different accounts or theories of representation: the reflective, the intentional and the constructionist. The reflective approach involves how language reflects a meaning which already exists out there in the real world of objects, people and events. The intentional approach explores the personal intended meaning of the meaning making agents (e.g. the speaker, the writer, or the painter). The constructionist approach is concerned with how meaning is constructed in and through language. This approach stresses the sociolinguistic construction of particular social issues, such as class, gender, ethnicity, identity, instance, stereotyping, bias, or prejudice, which have been materialised and mediated through language use. In this book, the constructionist approach will be adopted to analyse the media representation of migrant workers in China.

In this chapter, the theories that underpin the sociolinguistic analyses of Chinese media discourse in this book are presented .They fall into four different interwoven categories or themes and will be reviewed sequentially. The first review covers the sociolinguistic theories that have been adopted to illuminate Chinese discourse analysis. This thread of review includes discussion of the traditional variationist sociolinguistic approach and recent interactional and sociocultural approaches. The second theme draws its foundational concepts from critical discourse analysis, including text, genre, discourse, and discursive event, and is an important base for the media discourse analysis in this book. The third theme involves discussion of previous theories on media discourse analysis and, in particular, the genre approach to media discourse. Here, media narrative is considered as a text type or genre as well as a discursive activity or practice. The fourth review draws from the literature examining the sociolinguistic construction of identity and stance in media discourse and considers how identity and stance have been constructed and mediated linguistically in media discourse.

2.1. Sociolinguistic approaches to discourse studies

Sociolinguistics investigates the relationship between language and society. As its name suggests, it evolved as a multidisciplinary field (Coupland 2016) drawing from disciplines such as linguistics, sociology, psychology, anthropology, education, cultural studies, media studies, etc. It becomes a cover term for segments of different fields, such as variationist sociolinguistics, the social psychology of language, linguistic anthropology, the ethnography of communication, interactional sociolinguistics, linguistic ethnography, sociocultural linguistics, critical discourse analysis, etc. The variationist approach of sociolinguistics, first established by Labov (1963, 1966, 1972) and his followers, laid the foundation of sociolinguistics as an independent discipline. The key concerns of this approach (i.e. language variation, change, and structure) still remain important issues in contemporary linguistics research. Following that, sociolinguistics was extended with the developments of the anthropological approach by Hymes (1974; Gumperz and Hymes 1972) and interactional sociolinguistics by Gumperz (1982, 2001) among many other approaches. More recently, a sociocultural linguistic approach was initiated by Hall and Bucholtz (2005, 2008) with a view to distinguishing it from the traditional variationist sociolinguistics often associated with the quantitative analysis of linguistic features and their correlation to sociological variables. The term 'sociocultural linguistics' is currently used to promote a broadly interdisciplinary approach to language, culture and society.

The diverse approaches in sociolinguistics can be roughly put in a continuum which runs from 'socio' to 'linguistic' orientations. Each approach is aligned with some point of emphasis on this continuum. Its linguistic end covers examinations of language variation and change in phonological, lexical, and morphological levels, while its social end embraces research on societal bilingualism or multilingualism, language maintenance and shift, language contact, language ideology, and language planning, etc. This chapter particularly considers how variationist, interactional, and sociocultural approaches of sociolinguistics have contributed to the analysis of Chinese media discourse.

2.1.1. Variationist sociolinguistics

Sociolinguists widely attribute the seminal studies of language variation and change in the variationist approach to research conducted by William Labov (1963, 1966, 1969, 1972). Variationist sociolinguistics is concerned with linguistic variation and change in written and spoken language. While linguistic variation focuses on synchronic differences in speakers' pronunciation, word choice, morphology, or syntax, linguistic change examines diachronic developments of the language. The central ideas of this approach are that an understanding of language requires an understanding of variable as well as categorical processes and that variation at all levels of language is not random. This approach aims to uncover the correlation between language variation and social/cultural factors, such as ethnicity, religion, temporal and spatial differences, gender, age, level of education, occupation, etc.

In terms of research method, variationist sociolinguistics often features large scale quantitative studies examining correlations between language forms and language user variables. Contemporary variationist research has also extended its focus from the analysis of traditional aspects of linguistic variation and change, i.e. the phonological, morpho-syntactic, to discourse/pragmatic aspects, while incorporating contemporary quantitative methods and statistical practice.

Bell (1991) was among the first to draw on a sociolinguistic approach to analyse media discourse. In his frameworks of media discourse analysis, Bell emphasizes the importance of the processes which produce media language, as stories are constructed and modified by various hands. He stresses it is indeed stories or narratives that journalists and editors produce, not articles. These stories have viewpoint, values and structure that can be analysed. He is concerned, too, with the role of the audience in influencing media language styles, and in understanding, forgetting or misconceiving the news presented to it.

In Chinese contexts, the variationist approach was first introduced to mainland China in the late 1970s and 1980s (e.g. Zhu 1985; Chen 1985), and it has been consistently followed and promoted by a group of Chinese scholars in examining Chinese discourse. Chen's book (1999) is the first monograph in Chinese introducing theories of language variation and change systematically, discussing relevant research methods and applications of variationist sociolinguistics. Xu (2006) provides a comprehensive review of the variationist approach in western contexts, discussing new developments in the field and delineating the potential applications of these theories in Chinese contexts.

Replicating the research of language variation and change in western contexts, Chinese scholars have investigated variations and changes of Chinese as a result of social and technological development, language contact, and other factors, not only at the lexical level, but also at phonological, syntactic, pragmatic, and stylistic levels (e.g. Cao 2013; Su 2010). Drawing on this approach, scholars have also examined Chinese language and discourse in diverse social contexts. Xu and his colleagues employed this approach to investigate Chinese language variations in the city, for example, the use of *Putonghua*, Nanjing dialect, and other linguistic varieties by people of different genders and age in

Nanjing (Xu and Fu 2005; Xu and Wang 2010). Drawing on Labov's 'rapid anonymous observation', they designed the 'Asking-the-Way' data collection technique to collect street data of linguistic variation by asking people the way in the standard variety (i.e. *Putonghua*) (Xu and Fu 2005). This study finds that, though most interviewees' 'insider language' (i.e. language used to communicate with family, friends, and all acquaintances) is not Mandarin, nearly 100% of the interviewees accept Mandarin as the daily communication tool, especially as an 'outsider language' to communicate with strangers.

Zhang (2005) examined four phonological variables (i.e. rhotacization, lenition, interdental, full tone) among Chinese professionals in foreign and state-owned companies in Beijing. Her study demonstrated that professionals in foreign businesses employ linguistic resources from both local and global sources to construct a new cosmopolitan variety of Mandarin, whereas their counterparts in state-owned businesses favor the use of local features. This study shows that the linguistic practice of professionals in foreign companies in the local site of Beijing is inseparable from what is happening in the transnational Chinese community and the global market. They see themselves as belonging simultaneously to Beijing, mainland China, and the international business world. Their sense of flexible belonging is articulated through their linguistic behavior. This study indicates that the linguistic variation does not just reflect existing social categories and social change, but is a resource for constructing those categories and participates in social change.

However, while previous research in Chinese contexts has highly emphasized the linguistic variations and changes in terms of forms, types, and the sociocultural reasons behind these changes, more work needs to be done to uncover the patterns and structures of these variations and changes, and to explore the relationship between the variations/changes and the language structure, which has been regarded as the core of variationist sociolinguistics. Only with more in-depth empirical studies in this regard being carried out in Chinese contexts, can the research findings be better utilized to provide insights to Chinese discourse studies and policy making.

2.1.2. Interactional sociolinguistics

If we postulate that the variationist approach is aligned with the linguistic end of sociolinguistics, then the interactional approach is located in the middle of the social-linguistic continuum that explores how language is used to create meaning via social interactions. The work drawing on this approach includes research on participants, the norms of interaction and audience, and the social construction of meaning through language choices and changes. Unlike the variationist approach, interactional sociolinguistics, represented by John Gumperz (1982), extends the units of analysis to the larger context of language use and to larger stretches of language use such as conversations and texts. This approach is largely qualitative in nature and aims to combine wider contextual knowledge with linguistic analysis to illuminate the interpretive processes of interaction. Like other branches in sociolinguistics, interactional sociolinguistics bears a strong social/cultural agenda in its linguistic exploration. It works to demonstrate the connection between "small-scale interactions" and "large-scale sociological effects" (Jacquemet 2011:475), providing a "dynamic view of social environments where history, economic forces and interactive processes… combine to create or to eliminate social distinctions' (Gumperz 1982:29).

Although research methods used in interactional sociolinguistic research often blend tools and theories from pragmatics, conversation analysis, politeness and other linguistic theories, interactional sociolinguistics usually makes use of both ethnographic and linguistic methods to investigate language use in interaction (Gumperz 2001). The ethnographic research is often used at the initial stage of the research to provide insights into the local communication setting; to identify representative data relevant to the research question; and to check whether the analyst's expectations and interpretations are in line with or contrary to those of the local interlocutors. Following up on that, the researchers examine audio or video recordings of conversations or other interactions by drawing on various linguistic methods. They analyse linguistic forms such as words, sentences and even the whole text, as well as other subtle cues such as prosody and register that the interlocutors rely on in the communication process. Interactional sociolinguistics has been widely used in investigating linguistic interaction in various social settings and professional domains.

In the field of Chinese discourse studies in mainland China, interactional sociolinguistics was first introduced as a discourse analytical approach in early 2000s by Xu (2002), followed by a series of introductory and commentary publications in Chinese in the new century. In this newly emerging research field in China, an increasing number of empirical studies drawing on interactional sociolinguistics have been conducted to examine Chinese discourse and have been published as academic articles and research degree theses (e.g. Endo 2013; Pan and Kadar 2013; Wang, X. 2015; Zhu 2016). Pan and Kadar (2013) brought together empirical studies that employ diverse methods and analytic frameworks of interactional sociolinguistics in analysing data sources derived from various Chinese contexts, including mainland China, Hong Kong, Taiwan, Singapore and other overseas Chinese communities. In Pan and Kadar's (2013) collection, Endo (2013) examined the sentential positions and functions of a Chinese expression *wo juede* (Chinese: 我觉得, i.e. I think) and its relation to the epistemic stance that speakers take in conversation. The study found that Chinese speakers modulate social relation with their interlocutors by changing the positions of *wo juede* in conversation.

Wang, X. (2015) examined the supportive verbal feedback, such as some interjection or exclamation words like mh (嗯), ah (啊), yeah (对), or some nonverbal feedback signals like nodding, in naturally occurring Chinese conversation with a view to exploring the influence of social factors on supportive verbal feedback. That study investigated the form, pragmatic function and the distribution of verbal supportive feedback in Chinese natural conversations and discussed the interactive mechanism and characteristics of supportive feedback in the Chinese language.

Zhu (2016) investigated extended concurrent speech and *guanxi* (Chinese: 关系, i.e. relationship) management in Mandarin. Drawing on interactional sociolinguistics (incl. conversation analysis and ethnographic information concerning the participants' relational history, occupation, age, sex and social distance), this study explores extended concurrent speech as a strategy for *guanxi* management employed by non-familial equal-status Mandarin speakers in everyday practice. Spontaneous mundane conversations (i.e. 8 extracts) were analyzed and interpreted with the focuses on central linguistic features and marginalised contextualization cues, and situates inferences in contexts. The participants were found to co-construct extended concurrent speech to maintain or enhance *guanxi* without any manifestations of negative evaluation. The study suggests the importance of situating research in local and large contexts, and the necessity to examine extended concurrent speech, floor taking and topic switching in different varieties of Chinese.

In addition, Wu et al. (2016) review and critique a large number of sociolinguistic studies on new media during the recent decades and propose further directions for future research in this area of inquiry. More studies are expected to adopt this approach to analysing Chinese discourse occurring in diverse social settings.

2.1.3. Sociocultural linguistics

In the new century, due to disciplinary and methodological distinctions, the term 'sociolinguistics' has been crystalized to closely link to the variationist approach in sociolinguistics, which explores the correlation between language forms and language users variables with a large scale quantitative analysis (Shuy 2003; Spolsky 2010). In outlining current developments in socio-linguistic studies and their difference from the traditional variationist approach, Bucholtz and Hall (2005, 2008) advocate the use of the term 'sociocultural linguistics' to highlight the interdisciplinary efforts in exploring the interrelationship between language, individual, culture, and society. In the same vein, scholars in Europe talk about 'linguistic ethnography' (Blommaert 2005; Rampton et al. 2015) to emphasize the importance of incorporating ethnography into linguistic studies. These two schools, while sharing many commonalities, can be regarded as spearheading the current efforts of breaking down the traditional demarcation between anthropological and linguistic approaches to language. In the traditional sense, the anthropological approaches include interactional linguistics and seek to illuminate culture through investigation of speech events (e.g. Hymes 1974) and interactional practices (e.g. Gumperz 1982), whereas the linguistic approach largely draws on social information to address issues of linguistic structure, variation, and change (e.g. Labov 1966). In promoting a broadly interdisciplinary sociocultural approach to language and discourse, sociocultural linguistics manages to 'forge an alliance or coalition that fosters dialogue and collaboration between complementary approaches' (Bucholtz and Hall 2008: 403) in the investigation of language and discourse that will illuminate social and cultural processes.

As argued by Bucholtz and Hall (2008), the key strengths of sociocultural linguistics in terms of theories, methods, and issues include

- the ethnographic grounding of linguistic anthropology and the ethnomethodological sensibility of conversation analysis, which in different ways privilege the perspectives of participants over those of the analyst;
- the rigorous analytic tools of quantitative sociolinguistics and conversation analysis for the detailed investigation of linguistic and interactional structures;
- the attentiveness to texts and media of all kinds within critical discourse analysis as a necessary and often-ignored complement to the analysis of unmediated face-to-face interaction;
- a sociocultural focus on the content of discourse as well as a linguistic focus on its structure, and especially on the connection between these two;
- the attention to social theory found especially in linguistic anthropology; critical discourse analysis; language, gender, and sexuality studies; and U.K.-based sociolinguistics;
- the problem-solving orientation of applied linguistics coupled with the critical engagement and progressive-political commitment of critical discourse analysis; language, gender, and sexuality studies; and sociolinguistic and linguistic-anthropological research on minority languages and dialects. (Bucholtz and Hall 2008:423)

Similar to Bucholtz and Hall, Rampton and his colleagues (Rampton et al. 2015) describe linguistic ethnography as a 'discursive space' and 'a site of encounter' that brings together scholars with mixed interests and backgrounds in broad alignment with two basic tenets:

1) the contexts for communication should be investigated rather than assumed. Meaning takes shape within specific social relations, interactional histories and institutional regimes, produced and construed by agents with expectations and repertoires that have to be grasped ethnographically;
2) analysis of the internal organisation of verbal (and other kinds of semiotic) data is essential to understanding its significance and position in the world. Meaning is far more than just the 'expression of ideas', and biography, identifications, stance and nuance are extensively signalled in the linguistic and textual fine-grain. (Rampton et al. 2015:18)

Scholars drawing on sociocultural linguistics or linguistic ethnography generally hold that language and social life mutually shape each other, and that close analysis of situated language use can provide both fundamental and typical insights into the mechanisms and dynamics of social and cultural practices (Bucholtz and Hall 2005; Rampton et al. 2015).

In unravelling the intricate relation between language and society, contemporary developments in sociocultural linguistics and linguistic ethnography show increasing interest in small scale qualitative studies that incorporate ethnographic methods in their socio-cultural linguistic investigation (Rampton et al. 2015; Coupland and Jaworski 2009). This approach has been widely employed to explore socio/cultural issues, such as identity, gender, stance, membership, discrimination and injustice, which have materialised and been mediated through language use. This approach, concurring with the latest developments in media discourse studies, has also been employed in understanding media discourse and discourse practice.

2.2. Media discourse and critical discourse analysis

In light of the textual data collected and the research objectives of this book, some primary principles and concepts of critical discourse analysis (CDA thereafter) will also be employed for the data analysis. Critical discourse analysis (CDA) is a rapidly developing area of language study. It regards discourse as 'a form as social practice' (Fairclough and Wodak 1997: 258), and takes consideration of the context of language use to be crucial to discourse (Wodak 2001). It takes particular interest in the relation between language and power. CDA may be described as neo-Marxist; claiming that cultural and economic dimensions are significant in the creation and maintenance of power relations. The key figures in this area include Fairclough (1993, 1995, 2010, 2012), van Dijk (1998, 2011), and Wodak (2001). It is generally agreed that CDA cannot be classified as a single method but is rather viewed as an approach, which consists of different perspectives and different methods for studying the relationship between the use of language and social context.

The following are the key terms used in Fairclough's approach (Fairclough 1993, 1995, 2010, 2012) of CDA:

The first term that is crucial in the understanding of CDA is *text*, which in Fairclough's words refers to "the written or spoken language produced in a discursive event" (Fairclough 1993: 138). Fairclough emphasizes the multi-semiotic character of texts and adds visual images and sound – using the example of television language – as other semiotic forms which may be simultaneously present in texts.

Another key term is *genre*, which, for Fairclough, is "the use of language associated with a particular social activity" (Fairclough 1993: 138). For him, genre is also a means of textual structuring and a set of relatively stable conventions, which are both creative and conservative. That means that genre is both relatively stable and at the same time open to change.

Discourse, used as an abstract or uncountable noun, refers to "language use conceived as social practice" (Fairclough 1993: 138). When discourse is used as a concrete or countable noun, it refers to a "way of signifying experience from a particular perspective" (Fairclough 1993:

138). Fairclough further points out that the question of discourse is the question of how text figures (in relation to other moments) in how people represent the world, including themselves and their productive activities. Different discourses are different ways of representing associated with different positions (Fairclough 2000: 170).

Discourse, as an abstract noun, is not only concerned with language in use, but also the pervasive and often invisible sets of values, beliefs and ideas in that social circumstance.

A discursive event is an "instance of language use, analysed as text, discursive practice, social practice" (Fairclough 1993: 138). Discursive event, thus, refers to text, discursive practice (production and interpretation of the text), and social practice (including situational, institutional and societal practice).

Orders of discourse concern the "totality of discursive practices of an institution and relationship between them" (Fairclough 1993: 138). They are usually associated with particular institutions or domains of social life. For example, there are particular orders of discourse associated with schools. In describing orders of discourse, one is concerned with specifying what discourse types are used in the domain, and the relationships between each discursive practice (production and interpretation of discourse).

While orders of discourse are not rigid or closed, but open and changing, the core of an order of discourse is to foreground the different relationships between different discourse types (i.e. text types), and to investigate whether different text types in particular texts maintain strict boundaries or mix together. The same applies to the relationship between different orders of discourse. Different orders of discourse may overlap, blend together, or stay strictly within their own domain. Every discourse event (i.e. instance of language use) reproduces or challenges the order of discourse by creative use of language, such as absorbing different text types and discourses from other orders of discourse in a new way. The combination of different discourses and genres inside an order of discourse or across different orders of discourse results in the hybridity or heterogeneity of texts, or interdiscursivity in Fairclough's words (Fairclough 2010, 2015).

CDA sees the relationship between language and society as dialectical. This means that the relationship between language and society is two-way: on the one hand, language is influenced by society; on the other hand, society is shaped by language. Describing discourse as social practice implies that language and society bears a kind of dialectical relationship. This means that discourse constitutes situations, objects of knowledge and the identities of people. Discourse constitutes the social status quo and at the same time it is shaped by the situation.

According to Fairclough, language is not only socially constitutive but also socially shaped. The process of being socially shaped is a very complex one. On one hand very different types of discourses may coexist within the same institution, while on the other hand the relationship between the language use and the underlying conventions and norms is not always a simple linear one (Fairclough 2010). The term 'mediation' has been widely employed to describe the relation between language use and society, which means that the relationship of language and society is not direct, and language or discourse is just the medium to bring out values, beliefs, conventions and norms of society.

Critical discourse analysis considers the relationship between language use and wider social and cultural structures. In Fairclough's term this means the relationships between a specific communicative event, such as newspaper coverage of an event, and the total structure of an order of discourse, as well as modifications to the order of discourse and its constituents, genres and discourses (Fairclough 2010, 2015).

The structural changes in orders of discourse are inextricably associated with conflicts and struggles on societal and institutional levels. As to Fairclough (2010), the restructuring of boundaries inside and between the orders of discourse is a reflection of power struggle and the changes of social culture on the level of discourse. The creative discursive practices of blending different genres and discourses are not only the signs of discourse and social cultural changes, but also are the driving force of discourse and social cultural changes (Fairclough 2010, 2015; Bakhtin 1986; Bhatia 2004). These insights require analysts to incorporate elements of context into the analysis of texts so as to show the relationship between detailed linguistic features and the processes of social change on a broader scale.

2.3. Media discourse: genre and narrative

Media are everywhere in today's world, and China is no exception. People's lives are surrounded by newspapers, magazines, televisions, radios, the Internet, movies, books, and more recently, various social media, in particular, WeChat and Sina *Weibo*. In analysing types of media discourse in different media, this book will draw on a genre approach to media discourse analysis.

2.3.1. A genre approach to media discourse

Genre (the French word for kind or type) has been defined in different ways in the field of applied linguistics. The most influential definitions are from three different traditions of genre studies. The first definition is from the tradition of rhetoric genre studies (RGS) (Schryer 2011). This school of scholarship has been influenced in particular by a paper written by the speech communications specialist (Miller 1984) titled 'Genre as social action', in which she argues for genre as rhetorical action based on recurrent situations and for an open principle of genre classification based on rhetorical practice, rather than a closed one based solely on structure, substance, or aim. Genre studies in this tradition focus less on features of the text and more on relations between text and context often by employing ethnographic research or case study methods. The second definition of genre is proposed by Martin from the perspective of systemic functional linguistics (SFL). Martin (1984:25) describes genre as "a staged, goal-orientated, and purposeful social activity that people engage in as members of their culture". The third is from English for Specific Purposes (ESP) proposed by Swales (1990), who defines genre as a class of communicative events with some shared set of communicative purposes. These purposes are recognised by members of the professional or academic community in which the genre occurs, and thereby constitute the rationale for the genre. This definition is extremely influential in ESP work on genre analysis. SFL and ESP traditions of genre studies put much emphasis on identifying structural elements in texts and make statements about the patterning of these elements.

These approaches to the analysis of genres have much in common, with considerable overlap, even though they deal with different issues and sometimes have different theoretical concerns. Bhatia (2004) summarized some of the common ground of genre studies as follows.

1) Genres are recognizable communicative events, characterised by a set of communicative purposes identified and mutually understood by members of the professional or academic community in which they regularly occur.
2) Genres are highly structured and conventionalised constructs, with constraints on allowable contributions not only in terms of the intentions one would like to give expression to and the shape they often take, but also in terms of the lexico-grammat ical resources one can employ to give discoursal values to such formal features.
3) Established members of a particular professional community will have a much greater knowledge and understanding of the use and exploitation of genres than those who are apprentices, new members or outsiders.
4) Although genres are viewed as conventionalised constructs, expert members of the disciplinary and professional communities often exploit generic resources to express not only 'private' but also organisational intentions within the constructs of 'socially recognized communicative purposes'.
5) Genres are reflections of disciplinary and organisational cultures, and in that sense, they focus on social actions embedded within disciplinary, professional and other institutional practices.
6) All disciplinary and professional genres have integrity of their own, which is often identified with reference to a combination of textual, discursive and contextual factors. (Bhatia 2004:23)

Based on the understanding of the three traditions of genre theory, Bhatia (2004) put forward a comprehensive definition of genre.

> Genre essentially refers to language use in a conventionalised communicative setting in order to give expression to a specific set of communicative goals of a disciplinary or social institution, which give rise to stable structural forms by

> imposing constraints on the use of lexico-grammatical as well as discoursal resources. (Bhatia 2004:23)

In print media discourse, genres might include news reports or stories, editorials, investigative reports, and commentaries, while media text types characterise texts in terms of rhetorical functions such as expository, argumentative, and narrative. For further explications of the differences between genre and text type see Martin (1997) and Paltridge (1996).

Based on the categorisation of media discourse set forth by Martin and Peters (1985), Hoey (1983) and White (2016), this book proposes a classification of media discourse that intends to capture basic text types and social functions of the media discourse under examination. Table 2.1 shows the text types and social functions that are identified in this book.

Text types	Functions
Media narrative	To report on a connected events, or to simply tell a story
Media expository	To explain what/how/why, or to persuade something is the case
Media argumentative	To question, argue against, or challenge an existing opinion on an issue of public interest
Hybrid	Any combined or mixed form of the above

Table 2.1. Text types and functions of the media discourse in Chinese media (based on Martin and Peters (1985), Hoey (1983) and White (2016)).

This categorisation of text types in media discourse captures basic modes of thought and ways of communication in media discourse. While narratives hold a personal and emotive tone, expository and argumentative texts usually signify being 'rational' and objective. This book will focus on narrative, the most commonly-used text type in media discourse, to investigate the media representation of migrant workers in China.

2.3.2. Media narrative

Narratives are everywhere. They exist in nearly every aspect of human communication such as myths, fables, legends, epic, history, movies, novels, poems, dramas, conversation, interviews, and meetings. In media discourse, narrative exists in news reports, opinion articles, TV talk shows, feature programs, blogs, and more... As argued by Barthes (1977:79), "Narrative ... is able to be carried by articulated language, written or spoken, fixed or moving images, gestures, and the ordered mixing of all these substances".

In discourse studies, sociolinguistics and anthropology, narrative is considered as the 'basic', most 'essential', mode of human communication. It is experience-as-told and as made social (Ochs and Capps 1996 provide an overview). Narrative is a basic human way of making sense of the world. As Riessman (1993) argues, people are leading 'storied lives'. In other words, narrative is constitutive of reality as well as of identity and subjectivity. Furthermore, Connelly and Clandinin (2006:477) proposed that, "story ... is a portal through which a person enters the world". This idea of story as a portal to experience means that people encounter every experience in the context of a web of historical meaning and significance. We call this web of meaning and significance 'story'.

Nevertheless, there is still no agreed definition of narrative. Labov (1972) describes narratives as stories about specific past events and they have a beginning, middle and end. Labov's framework (Labov and Waletzky 1967) suggests that stories should follow a chronological sequence and the order cannot be changed.

However, Young (1987) argued that the links between events may not always be chronological and Bakhtin (1981) claimed that narrative may not be formatted by time, but by episodes. By analysing perceptions of narratives, Riessman (1993, 2008) expects temporally sequenced plots, with attempts to hear and understand organized episodes. Generally, narratives are understood as stories that include an event or several events in a chronological order and in an effort to make something out of those events (Sandelowski 1991).

While narrative is regarded as a privileged window on human experience, Hymes (1996) insists that narrative is a universal function of language. But because of its deep context-embeddedness, its often 'irrational' or emotive key, and its connection to non-generalisable individual experience, it has been overlooked as a format of knowledge production and reproduction (Blommaert 2005:84).

In Fludernik's definition,

> A narrative … is a representation of a possible world in a linguistic and/or visual medium, at the centre of which there are one or more protagonists of an anthropomorphic nature who are existentially anchored in a temporal or spatial sense and who (mostly) perform goal directed actions (action and plot structure). It is the experience of these protagonists that narratives focus on, allowing readers to immerse themselves in a different world and in the life of the protagonists. (Fludernik 2009:6)

In such a perspective, conversational and written (literary/non-literary) narratives are not as far apart as they may seem, since the focus is not on events and actions per se but on the way humans experience and react to them.

In the field of media studies, quite a few works (e.g. Fulton et al. 2005; Ryan 2004, 2010) discuss and apply current narrative theories to print media texts, broadcasting programs, and even advertising. Drawing on research in structuralist and post-structuralist theories, these scholars explore how narrative techniques have shaped media texts and have offered interpretive tools for analysing meaning and ideology. They investigate particular media forms and show how elements such as chronology, character and focalisation are realised in specific texts.

2.3.3. Narrative as text

The best known linguistic analysis of oral narrative is that of Labov, in which he proposed a narrative structure, developed in a series of studies (Labov and Waletzky 1967; Labov 1972; Labov and Fanshel 1977). The main focus in this tradition which closely associates with structuralism is on the systematic description of the formal features that characterise narrative as a genre or text-type.

Labov is the founder of the discipline of variationist sociolinguistics. The key contributions he made in narrative analysis include two main aspects. One is narrative structure and the other 'evaluation'. Labov (1972) describes narratives as stories about specific past events and they have a beginning, middle and end. Labov's framework (Labov and Waletzky 1967) suggests that stories should follow a chronological sequence and the order cannot be changed.

Structure	Function
Abstract	What was this about?
Orientation	Who? When? What? Where?
Complication	Then what happened?
Evaluation	So what?
Result	What finally happened?
Coda	Signal the end of the narrative and form a bridge out of the story time

Table 2.2. Structure of a narrative (6 stages) (Based on Cortazzi 1993:45).

Evaluation is considered by Labov (1972) to be "perhaps the most important element in addition to the basic narrative clause". According to Labov, evaluation refers to "the means used by the narrator to indicate the point of the narrative", or to justify the claims in the 'abstract'. Evaluative devices indicate what was "terrifying, dangerous, weird, wild, crazy; or amusing, hilarious and wonderful... that is, worth reporting". Evaluative devices include direct statements, but more importantly, they include 'secondary structures' throughout the narrative. These structures consist of responses to the action presented as part of the story, intensifying devices both of sound and word choice, such as repetition, etc.

This insight has been further developed in recent work on subjectivity, evaluation and positioning in discourse (e.g. Thompson and Hunston 2000) and stance (Englebreton 2007; Bois 2007; Jaffe 2009) and appraisal theory in SFL (Martin and White 2007).

2.3.4. Narrative as interactional practice

The recent research in narrative analysis has theorised narrative as a discursive activity. That accounts for narrative as a contextually bound phenomenon and as a process that relates in specific ways to the life of linguistic and social communities.

Discourse and sociolinguistic narrative analysis has witnessed a shift from a long-standing conception of narrative (oral, natural, non-literary) as a well-defined and described genre with an identifiable structure toward an exploration of the multiplicity, fragmentation, and irreducible situatedness of its forms and functions in a wide range of social arenas (De Fina and Georgakopoulou 2012).

Narrative analysis from discourse and sociolinguistic perspectives has produced insights into how stories are structured (i.e. their formal features), into what makes stories tellable (i.e. cultural resonance and meaningfulness), into what kind of work is involved in how stories are told (i.e. their interactional design and situated tellings).

According to De Fina and Georgakopoulou (2008), there are three distinct elements in this shift. First, there is an increasing acceptance of narrative as a discursive activity informed by conversation analysis, ethnography of communication, linguistic anthropology, and interactional sociolinguistics. Second, there is an emphasis, derived from recent theories of context and genre (e.g. Bauman 2001), not just on the contextualised but also on the contextualising aspects of narrative. The notion of context remains elusive, contested, and indeterminate, but there is now consensus on the view of context not as a static surrounding frame but as a set of multiple and intersecting processes that are mutually interacting with text. In that vein, context is no longer considered as a pre-existing 'setting' that may be conventionally associated with certain kinds of language use and norms, but it becomes a dynamic notion of social spaces, prone to heterogeneity and fragmentation. This change has been instrumental in looking at narrative tellings in situ in ways in which space is more or less subtly referred to, reworked, and constructed anew within narrative plots. Third, there is an increasing commitment to social theoretical concerns (mainly within the framework of cultural studies). This is particularly evident in proliferating work on narrative and identities that has variously problematized, de-essentialised, or added nuance to the widely held view that narrative is a privileged communication mode for making sense of the self. Research in this area has also blurred the boundaries between narrative analysis and narrative inquiry, thus shifting the emphasis of the former from narrative as an end to narrative as a means to an end.

Narrative analysis can be the study of any type of narrative found in the private, public or political realms, including 'naturally occurring' narratives, oral or written narratives collected for research purposes, and narratives in public/policy documents or media texts. According to De Fina and Georgakopoulou (2012), research focuses in narrative analysis can range from examining narratives as texts/genres or as communicative or interactional processes to examining identities or social phenomena represented in narratives. As argued by the key scholars in narrative research (e.g. Mishler 1986; Reissman 2008; Clandinin 2007), narrative analysis is experience centred and can be culturally oriented. That means narrative analysis situates narratives in their social, cultural, political, and historical context, and can reveal qualities of individual/group experience that other methods cannot. If designed properly, narrative analysis and inquiry has the potential to level power dynamics, and benefit the research participants.

2.4. Media discourse, identity and stance

In the modern world, the media are involved in the production of identities and stances all the time. People understand the world by reading newspapers, magazines and books (both hard and digital copies), watching television, browsing webpages, and listening to the radio. The media tell people who are who and what others are doing in the world. The audience usually accepts what the media claim as true and authentic about the world. The media available in a specific area actually set boundaries for the people regarding how they are able to understand the world. In doing that, the media might be considered the most important producers of meaning and codes of meaning in contemporary society. However, when the media are re-presenting the world, they inevitably bring their own values, ideologies, beliefs and stances into this meaning making process. The media are then trying to get people to see the world according to the terms or codes that have been set by one or more groups of people, usually those who control the power within a society (Fowler 1991; Grossberg et al. 2006). The media operating in different parts of the world and by different people can represent the world very differently. Thus, the media become powerful ideological institutions and potentially become a source of great conflict and struggle.

2.4.1. Media and identity

The media provide pictures of people, describing different social groups and their identities. There are two main streams of thought concerning how people's identity is represented in mass media (Hall 2013). The first is an essentialist view that assumes media representation of identity can take the form of offering a natural, separate, and fully constituted identity. The second is an anti-essentialist view that rejects the assumptions of the first. This latter theory emphasises the impossibilities of representing such a fully constituted, separate and distinct identity. It argues that the categories of identity are culturally constructed and are always in process and change. In this sense, the media representation of identity is always manipulated and operationalized by the media in a way that can be controlled by the institutional ideology that the media have to follow.

For the analysis of identity as constituted in linguistic interaction, Bucholtz and Hall (2005) proposed a framework with the key principle that identity is the product rather than the source of linguistic and other semiotic practices. The sociocultural linguistic perspective on identity holds that identity is fundamentally a social and cultural phenomenon that emerges from linguistic and other semiotic practices. Identity in this framework is not simply viewed as a psychological mechanism of self-classification that is reflected in people's social behaviour but rather as something that is constituted through social action, and especially through language (Bucholtz and Hall 2005:588). In the context of media discourse analysis, it is presumed that the identity represented in the media is the product that emerges from the interaction between the media subjects (i.e. those about whom the media discourse is talking), the journalists, and even the audience.

Bucholtz and Hall (2005) also discuss and illustrate an important pair of concepts – adequation and distinction – in linguistic identity research. According to them, adequation emphasises the fact that in order to be positioned as alike, individuals or groups must be understood as sufficiently similar in any interaction which might index identity. In this kind of interaction, differences irrelevant or destructive to any efforts to adequate two people or groups will be played down. As the counterpart of adequation, distinction, originally conceptualised by Pierre Bourdieu (1984), is concerned with the production of social-class difference by members of the bourgeoisie. Bucholtz and Hall (2005) broaden its reference to include any process of social differentiation. Because language is an extremely important resource for producing social differentiation, the analysis of discourse or language used in this social process becomes a vital area of sociocultural linguistic research on identity.

In the context of Chinese society, Pun (1999) reported a year-long ethnographic study examining *Dagong Mei* (i.e. female migrant workers) based in Guangdong. Focusing on a shift in the *Dagong Mei*'s identities in light of China's attempt to enter the world economy, Pun's study reveals that as women, as peasants and as migrant workers, the ambiguous and overlapping identities of the *Dagong Mei* elucidate how the party-state, the capitalist market and China's patriarchal culture work hand in hand to produce new relations of power and domination. It is argued that new social identities are created for these women, taking advantage of rural-urban disparities, and regional and gender inequalities.

2.4.2. Media and stance

Stance, as defined by Bois (2007:163), is "a public act by a social actor, achieved dialogically through overt communication means (language, gesture, and other symbolic forms), through which social actors simultaneously evaluate objects, position subjects (themselves and others), and align with other subjects, with respect to any salient dimension of the sociocultural field". From linguistic or sociolinguistic perspectives, there are various terms that have been used to describe different types of stance-taking, such as footing, alignment, positioning, and addressivity (see Jaffe 2009 for a detailed summary). Bois (2007:139) argues that stance is "one of the most important things we do with words," and it is "a linguistically articulated form of social action". In theorising and operationalizing stance analysis, perhaps the most well-known is Bois' (2007) stance triangle (Figure 2.1), which is a geometric model that visually represents interrelations between three elements of stance-taking.

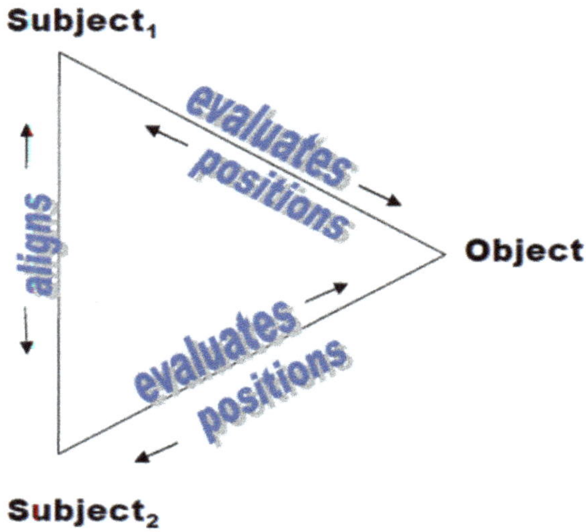

Figure 2.1. The stance triangle by Bois (2007).

In the above triangle, Bois has developed a framework that highlights the relationship between current author (subject 1), prior author (subject 2), and stance object. He uses the 'stance triangle' as a tool for attending to "the structured interrelations among the acts and entities which comprise stance (and thus allow) participants, and analysts, to draw inferences by triangulating from the explicit components of stance to the implicit" (Bois 2007:165). Bois argues that we simultaneously accomplish several component acts in a single act of stance-taking. First, he takes up these component acts individually, testing the possibility that there are several different types of stance, before arguing that each is a component part of a single act of stance-taking. He defines evaluation, also known as assessment or appraisal, as "the process whereby a stancetaker orients to an object of stance and characterises it as having some specific quality or value" (Bois 2007:143); that is, the emphasis is on the supposedly inherent qualities of the object of the stance. In contrast, positioning puts the focus on stancetaker 2 whose position is composed of both affective stance (typified by an affective predicate in a sentence such as "I'm glad") and epistemic stance, or claim to variable degrees of certainty or knowledge. The third aspect of stance-taking is alignment, "the act of calibrating the relationship between two stances, and by implication between two stancetakers" (Bois 2007: 144).

Thus Bois explains stance-taking, using the first-person point of view of the stancetaker: "I evaluate something, and thereby position myself, and thereby align with (respect to) you" (Bois 2007: 163). This formulation emphasizes three crucial entities in stance-taking: the present stancetaker (Subject 1); a prior stancetaker (Subject 2), with whom Subject 1 aligns; and a stance object to which both stancetakers are oriented.

2.5. Media discourse analysis in Chinese contexts

In light of the theories reviewed above, this book will steer from examination of media narratives as texts to exploration of the narratives as interactional activities with a view to unravelling how the media in China portray identities of this socially disadvantaged group, how different social members express their stances towards this group through media, and how the public media build up the migrant workers' identities and manipulate the construction process in an attempt to counterbalance the pervasive social discourses.

This book draws on the sociocultural linguistic perspective on identity (Bucholtz and Hall 2005, 2008; Bucholtz 1999, 2002), narrative identity research (Benwell and Stokoe 2006; Daiute and Lightfoot 2004; De Fina and Georgakopoulou 2008, 2012), stancetaking and positioning theories (Bois 2007; Jaffe 2009), as well as Goffman's dramaturgical analysis (1956,1974) and many other social theories, which together provide the researcher with a repertoire of tools for conceptualising, analysing and interpreting the data.

For the analysis of identity as constituted in linguistic interaction, sociocultural linguistic researchers on identity hold that identity is the product rather than the source of linguistic and other semiotic practices. They claim that identity is fundamentally a social and cultural phenomenon that emerges from linguistic and other semiotic practices. Identity in this research tradition is not simply viewed as a psychological mechanism of self-classification that is reflected in people's social behaviour but rather as something that is constituted through social action, and especially through language (Bucholtz and Hall 2005: 588).

This book is concerned with how the identities of and stances towards migrant workers have been constructed and mediated in public media (e.g. newspapers, magazines and TV programs) in China and what is the relationship between media representation of migrant workers and social change in contemporary China. The objectives of the book include, first, to explore the interrelationship between media representation of migrant workers and social change in contemporary China; second, to examine how identities of migrant workers have been constructed, transformed and mediated in China's media discourse; third, to analyse stances towards migrant workers represented in Chinese media with a focus on investigation of ways in which agents or agencies manipulate this sociolinguistic construction.

The book sets out to constitute a conceptual advance in understanding one of the most noteworthy components of the Chinese population against a backdrop of high mobility in China. It provides a comprehensive study on how the media representation of migrant workers is interacting with the sociocultural transformation in China. The findings and discussions of the book will shed critical insights into further research on migrant workers in China and media discourse in contemporary Chinese society.

3. Newspaper representation of migrant workers in China

Taking a sample of six influential Chinese newspapers, this chapter examines the representation of Chinese internal migrant workers in the public media in China. The newspapers selected are *People's Daily, Jiefang Daily, Southern Daily, Beijing Times, Xinmin Evening News* and *Southern Metropolis Daily*. These six newspapers from the three major cities in China: Beijing, Shanghai and Guangzhou, were chosen to represent leading newspapers geographically. Drawing on discourse analysis and sociolinguistic theories, this chapter illustrates how migrant workers have been framed and represented in the Chinese media with the aim of revealing diverse socio-political viewpoints on and stances towards this distinctive social group. The themes covered in these newspapers range over topics such as integration of the migrant workers into urban life, social welfare of the migrants, self-development of the migrants, the non-payment or withholding of their wages, and the education of the migrants' children.

In addition to their geographic representativeness, these newspapers were also chosen to exemplify the two major types of newspapers in China, namely, the party's traditional mouthpieces (all broadsheets), represented by *People's Daily, Jiefang Daily* and *Southern Daily*, and the newly emerged tabloid styled local newspapers, here represented by *Beijing Times, Xinmin Evening News* and *Southern Metropolis Daily*. These two types of newspapers differ significantly from each other in terms of funding sources, social issues covered, perspectives taken, media strategies, and readership targets. This chapter starts with a brief introduction to newspapers in mainland China with a focus on the six newspapers. It then provides a critical review of previous studies analysing identities of migrant workers in China. The core part of the chapter is an examination of how the identities of migrant workers have been represented in these newspapers and a discussion of how these analyses contribute to existing scholarship.

3.1. Newspapers in China

The landscape of China's newspapers is complex but it can be roughly categorised into two major levels, i.e. national and regional (Wang 2007). National newspapers, published by major agencies of the party or the government, aim to exert nationwide influence on issues of public interest, while regional newspapers are locally based in the provinces or cities with a focus on local affairs with limited influence on the whole country. For example, general national newspapers such as *People's Daily* and *Guangmin Daily*, mainly based in Beijing, are circulated to fulfil the party's commitments. Regional papers include Shanghai-based *Jiefang Daily* and *Wenhui Daily*, Guangzhou-based *Southern Daily, Southern Metropolis Daily,* and *Southern Weekend*, and all the many newspapers published in local provinces and cities. At the national level, there are also newspapers targeting audiences in specific fields or industries. These 'national specialist newspapers' include such publications as *Fazhi Ribao* (Legal Daily) – supervised by the Ministry of Justice, *Nongmin Ribao* (Farmers' Daily) concerning agricultural and rural issues, and *Jiefangjun Bao* (PLA Daily) – the official daily of the People's Liberation Army. As a legacy of the former planned economy system in China, every industry sector or national administrative organ tends to publish its own field-specific print outlet to cover news and reports concerning that specific sector.

In terms of format, following western media tradition, Chinese newspapers can be described in binary terms as either 'broadsheet' or 'tabloid'. Those formats originally had implications of 'seriousness' attached to the former and 'populism' and 'sensationalism' to the latter. Conventionally, these labels have also been correlated respectively with the party-state run newspapers and the commercialised ones, with the party-state newspapers most likely being broadsheet and the commercialised newspapers tending to follow the tabloid format. Typical examples include the broadsheet provincial or municipal daily newspapers run by the party-state and the tabloid commercial morning or evening city newspapers (Chinese：都市报) published in every major city. However, these characterisations are no longer entirely accurate regarding tabloids. For example*, Global*

Times (Chinese: 环球时报) and *Reference News* (Chinese: 参考消息), both very influential party-run newspapers, follow a tabloid format. This might be partially due to the recent financial pursuits by media institutions in China. Along with the marketization of the economic system in China, the traditional media once fully sponsored by the State government have lost part of their financial support and have been forced to seek financial benefits on their own. This has forced them to shift their attention from political correctness to catering for the interests of the audience and, more crucially, pursuing their own financial rewards. Consequently, some previous 'serious' party-run newspapers have transformed to tabloids with the aim of attracting a higher circulation rate.

The details of the six Chinese newspapers selected to be included in this study are set out below.

Newspaper	**Level and location**	**Format**	**Key features**
People's Daily (人民日报)	National, Beijing	Broadsheet	The Central CPC's key organ
Jiefang Daily (解放日报)	Regional, Shanghai	Broadsheet	The key organ of the CPC Shanghai Commission
The *Southern Daily* (南方日报)	Regional, Guangzhou	Broadsheet	The key organ of the CPC Guangdong Commission
Beijing Times (京华时报)	Regional, Beijing	Tabloid	The key local tabloid newspaper in Beijing, formerly a part of the *People's Daily* Group and detached in 2012
Xinmin Evening News （新民晚报）	Regional, Shanghai	Tabloid	The key local tabloid newspaper in Shanghai, a part of the newly established Shanghai United Media Group
Southern Metropolis Daily (南方都市报)	Regional, Guangzhou	Tabloid	The key tabloid newspaper in Guangzhou, a part of the Southern Media Group

Table 3.1. Newspapers examined in this chapter.

Among all the newspapers published in China, *People's Daily* (Chinese: 人民日报) occupies a unique niche. As an organ of the Central Committee of the Communist Party of China (CPC), it provides direct information on the policies and viewpoints of the party. It claims to be viewed by UNESCO as "one of the 10 most authoritative and most influential newspapers of the world". As the party mouthpiece, *People's Daily* was fully sponsored by the party-state until the 1990s. Even until 2003, a subscription to *People's Daily* was mandatory for all government agencies and state-owned enterprises (Akhavan-Majid 2004). Functioning as the official ideological apparatus, *People's Daily* usually sets the tone for all other media in China. While its influence on Chinese society has shrivelled substantially, it is still endowed with the power to control public opinion. Concerning social issues such as internal migration, *People's Daily* might arguably hold the mission of reconciling the social tensions that exist between established city residents and the migrants, while promotion of a positive image of the migrant workers becomes one of the predictable strategies taken to fulfil that aim. The strategies taken to do so will be further discussed in the following sections.

Beijing Times started as a tabloid style paper and a part of the *People's Daily* group in 2001. In 2012, it became independent from the *People's Daily* group and demonstrated a strong circulation increase. It became one of the commercialised papers emerging in the early 2000s, enjoying a high circulation rate among local people in Beijing and beyond.

At the provincial or city level, Shanghai and Guangzhou based newspapers have been chosen because both of these two cities are at the hub of hosting migrant workers from inland and remote areas. Every year Beijing, Shanghai and Guangzhou are the top cities hosting millions of migrant workers from all over the country, who attempt to seek a better life in big metropolises. *Jiefang Daily* (Chinese: 解放日报) is the leading daily run by the Shanghai Municipal Committee of the Communist Party and is widely read by the general public. Another Shanghai-based newspaper, *Xinmin Evening News* (Chinese: 新民晚报) is a tabloid format paper, published since September 1929 in Shanghai. It is now owned by the newly established Shanghai United Media Group. Its current editorial mission as claimed on its website is the socialist-inspired mantra *"promote the policies from the government, spread the knowledge, change the culture, and enrich life"* (Chinese: 宣传政策, 传播知识, 移风易俗, 丰富生活).

In Guangzhou, the *Southern Daily* (Chinese: 南方日报) is the official Guangdong Communist Party newspaper, sister to the more lively and commercial *Southern Metropolis Daily* (Chinese: 南方都市报) and part of the giant Southern Media Group. This Guangzhou-based family of papers is known to possess superior reporting strategies and a higher level of frankness than many PRC mainstream press outlets. Following a tabloid format, *Southern Metropolis Daily* is well known for its investigative reporting and provocative commentaries, which often get it into trouble with the Beijing authorities. Its circulation is mainly in the Pearl River Delta area, containing Guangzhou, Shenzhen, Hong Kong and Macau, but its news stories and especially its investigative reports are much reprinted in many smaller regional newspapers. As one of the flagship media outlets in South China, *Southern Metropolis Daily* strives for excellence in providing its audience with unbiased and investigative reports on current affairs of general interest. With a daily circulation of about 1.8 million copies, the newspaper aims to 'be the best newspaper in China'. The target audience of this newspaper consists mainly of social elites and white-collar workers aged between 25 to 44 years, and more than half of them have completed tertiary education (Baidu 2017b).

This chapter will present analyses focussing on how these six newspapers represent the migrant workers, what the differences between them are, and why.

3.2. Media discourses about migrant workers and previous studies

Since the early 1980s and the advent of 'reform and opening', the media have named migrant workers *Nongmin Gong* or *Dagong Zai/Mei* which, all across China, literally means peasant workers/labourers.

Implicit in these terms is a strongly derogative stigmatization, due to the fact that there is a long tradition in China that peasants live at the lower end of the socio-political spectrum of society. Although migrants have made a great contribution to China's development, their integration into cities has not been warmly welcomed by local governments or established city residents. This phenomenon is evidenced by the terms used to label them in public media discourse (see details in Chapter 1 of this book). They have often been regarded as 'the other' or 'abnormal' individuals, as for a long time they have been viewed by the city dwellers as merely providers of cheap labour without proper social identification papers. Throughout the long period of their massive immigration into the urban areas, this social group has been unable to obtain the city *hukou* (household registration), which has prevented them from getting equal social status to city residents (as described in Chapter 1).

In the context of the public image of 'otherness' attached to the term *Nongmin Gong*, the party-state leaders and state-run media have recently attempted to provide a counter-discourse by tempering the perception of abnormality of migrant workers and advocating their normality. In their effort to curb discrimination and promote the integration of migrant workers into urban social life, State leaders and governments at various levels adopted the terms *Xin Shimin* (新市民, new city residents) and *Xin Gongren* (新工人, new workers) for this social group. *Xin Shimin* was first used in 2006 and has been used cautiously by both the government and the public media since then. Although the terms *Nongmin Gong*, *Xin Shimin*, *Xin Gongren*, are based on real aspects of their personal identities (i.e. peasant, worker, new city-residents, etc.), whether these names are used and which points are highlighted depends much on the manipulation of public opinion by the media, and the government.

However, a search on Baidu Trends (i.e. a top keywords and high search volume keywords tool, to see which keywords are performing well in public media and Baidu search) shows that *Nongmin Gong* is still more commonly used than *Xin Shimin* in people's everyday use and media discourse.

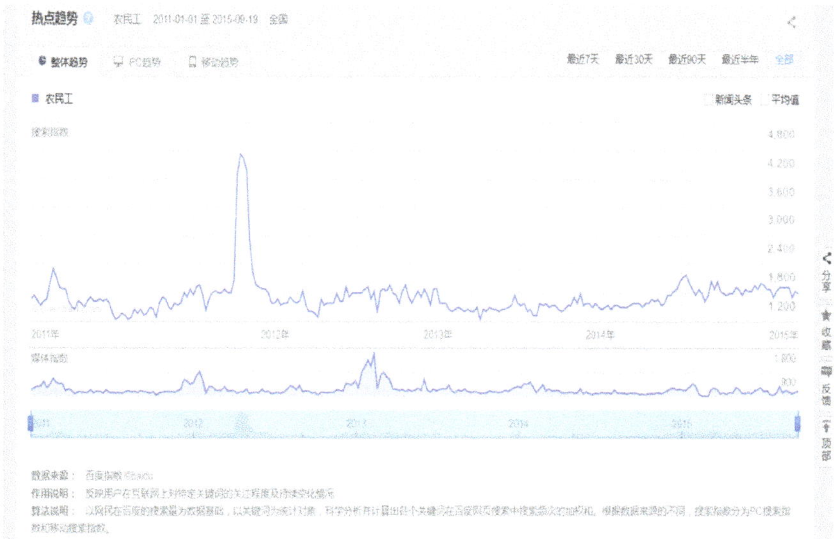

Figure 3.1. Baidu Trends in Searching *Nongmin Gong* from 1 January 2011 to 19 September 2015.

This figure indicates that the public search index of the term *Nongmin Gong* peaks in November/December 2011 and the media index of this term culminates in January 2013. The average search index of this term is above 1,200 per day, and the media index is in the range of 900 to 1,800 in this time period.

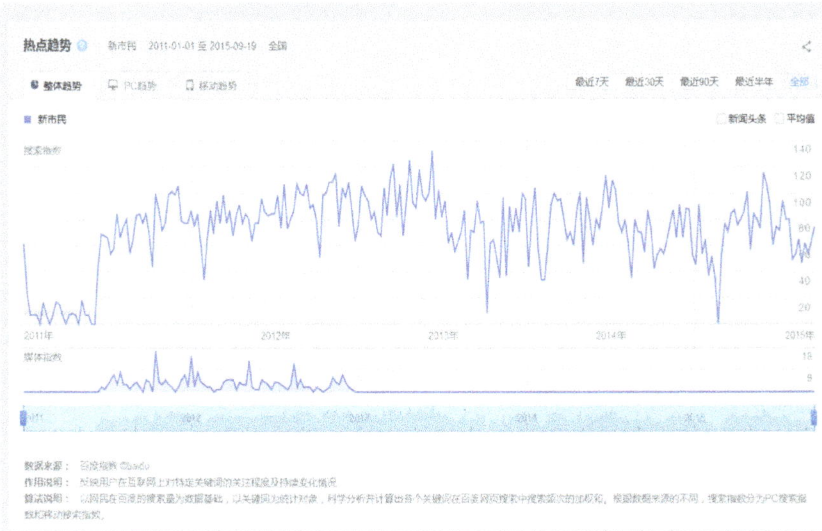

Figure 3.2. Baidu Trends in Searching *Xin Shimin* from 1 January 2011 to 19 September 2015.

Figure 3.2 indicates that the term *Xin Shimin* is far less popular than *Nongmin Gong* in both the search index and the media index. The average search volume fluctuates around 100 with a peak of about 130 at the end of 2012. The media index is around 9 to 18 and, after 2012, it is around 9. The term *Xin Gongren* encounters approximately the same situation.

The comparison of these two figures clearly indicates that until 2015 the term *Nongmin Gong* is steadily the key term used in both the public discourse and the media coverage in referring to the migrant workers in China. It seems to there will be a long way to go before any alteration in the public discourse naming of migrant workers will be apparent.

In the media studies field, there has been a couple of research projects investigating media representation of migrant workers in Chinese contexts. Li (2006, 2007) reports an interesting research project investigating how peasant workers (i.e. *Nongmin Gong*) have been represented in the local newspapers in China. Based on narrative analysis of news coverage of the migrant group in four Guangzhou-based dailies (i.e. *Southern Daily*, *Yangcheng Evening*, *Guangzhou Daily* and *Southern Metropolis Daily*), this project explores how China's urban print media portrayed this peasant immigrant group as different from mainstream urban dwellers in China. It also considers the implication and influences of the media portrayal upon the social identity formation of this group and its recognition by the urban cities. The research asserts that on the one hand, urban newspapers create spaces for the group to express its experiences and subjectivities by producing frequent 'suffering' narratives and 'suffering' images with a view to facilitating the urban members' cultural recognition of this group; on the other hand, the media's frequent representation of the group as "threat" and "trouble" through "negative" narratives hinders the group from being accepted culturally by urban groups.

In this research, Li also categorises the narratives about the migrant group published in the newspapers into five groups, i.e. 'victim' narratives, 'negative behaviour' narratives, 'hero/positive behaviour' narratives, 'being protected' narratives, and 'neutral' narratives. In addition, two hybrid narratives exist in the news reports, namely, the 'victim' plus 'negative behaviour' narrative and the 'victim' plus 'being protected' narrative. These highly stereotyped patterns have underpinned the news reports on migrant workers and have shaped the specific representations of the migrant workers in the public media in China. This study found that the most frequently used narrative patterns in three market-oriented newspapers (i.e. *Southern Metropolis Daily*, *Yangcheng Evening* and *Guangzhou Daily*) are 'victim' and 'negative behaviour' narratives. The party newspaper '*Southern Daily*' uses a slight different pattern by following the most frequently used patterns of 'being protected' and 'negative behaviour' narratives.

Chu (2010) investigates the framing of Chinese migrant workers in articles published in two Mainland Chinese newspapers and two Hong Kong newspapers from 2004 to 2009. Drawing on framing theory, this study reveals significant differences in the news frames between the two regions. Attribution of responsibility and morality are the most frequently used frames in Mainland newspapers, while human interest and responsibility frames dominate coverage in Hong Kong newspapers.

Government officials are the most popular sources cited by the four newspapers, followed by migrant workers. Media in both regions dealt with this issue using a fairly neutral tone, but had different attitudes towards the Chinese central government. Mainland news articles show a positive attitude, while Hong Kong journalists take a neutral stance. It is also found that the usage of frames, sources, and tone changed over the six-year period.

These prior studies have provided insights to assist the current research that investigates the newspaper representation of migrant workers across different regions and newspaper types in China.

3.3. Representation of migrant workers in the six newspapers in China

This section considers how the six newspapers represent the identities of and stances towards migrant workers in China. The primary data include all articles concerning migrant workers published from 1 January to 31 December 2014 in the six newspapers detailed above. The articles were collected through two main databases in China, i.e. the China Core Newspaper Database (CCND) published by China National Knowledge Infrastructure (CNKI) and Baidu News published by Baidu (roughly the Chinese version of Google). The full texts of *People's Daily* and *Southern Daily* were available from CCND and the full texts of the other four newspapers were collected from Baidu News. This chapter first identifies the articles in these six newspapers which use either the term '*Ningmin Gong*' or the terms '*Xin Shimin*/*Xin Gongren*'. The results are shown below in Table 3.2.

Newspaper	Articles concerning *Nongmin Gong* (农民工)	Articles concerning *Xin Shimin* or Xin Gongren (新市民或新工人)	Total
1.*People's Daily* (PD) (人民日报)	31	0	31
2.*Beijing Times* (BT) (京华时报)	35	10	45
3.*Jiefang Daily* (JD) (解放日报)	96	11	107
4.*Xinmin Evening News* (XEN) (新民晚报)	69	4	73
5.The *Southern Daily* (TSD) (南方日报)	5	0	5
6.*Southern Metropolis Daily* (SMD) (南方都市报)	17	0	17

Table 3.2. Numbers of articles concerning '*Nongmin Gong*' and '*Xin Shimin/Xin Gongren*' in the six newspapers in 2014.

The above table lists those articles using the terms '*Nongmin Gong*' and '*Xin Shimin* or *Xin Gongren*' in the six newspapers in 2014. These three terms convey subtly different ways of representing this newly emerging social group. In using *Nongmin Gong*, the hybrid nature of this group, i.e. peasants+ workers, is foregrounded, while both '*Xin Shimin*' and '*Xin Gongren*' attempt to conceal their peasant identity and highlight their new identity as either new city residents or workers. Concurring with the Baidu Trends searches, the data collected here clearly demonstrate that the term '*Nongmin Gong*' still predominates in representing this social group in the print media in contemporary China. There is certainly infrequent use of the term '*Xin Shimin*' in *Beijing Times*, *Jiefang Daily* and *Xinmin Evening News*, but surprisingly, there is no use at all of this term in *People's Daily*, *Southern Daily* and *Southern Metropolis Daily*. This denotes that, despite the strong advocacy of the state leaders, even the party's major mouthpiece '*People's Daily*' has not followed the directive seriously and still uses the term '*Nongmin Gong*' as the customary one to refer to this social group.

To explore the identities of migrant workers represented in the six newspapers, this chapter adopts the identity categorisation proposed by Grossberg et al. (2006: 220–221) and focuses on four major dimensions of people's identity:

1) Politically, people exist as citizens and as members of a public. This chapter considers whether the migrant workers are referred to as '*Nongmin Gong*' or '*Xin Shimin*/*Gongren*' in the news texts.
2) Socially, people exist as exemplars of social roles, such as fathers, children, sons and so on. This chapter considers which social roles are foregrounded in each text.
3) Culturally, people exist as exemplars of social groups. This chapter uses semiotic systems of differences, such as male or female, people from North or South of China.
4) Economically, people exist as consumers or paid workers. This chapter considers the exact job titles of the migrant workers as the key economical dimension.

These dimensions of migrant workers' identities in each news text collected for the study are examined and discussed below.

3.3.1. Identity dimensions of migrant workers foregrounded in the newspapers

Following Grossberg et al.'s framework, but merging cultural and social dimensions 2 and 3, Table 3.3 presents the summary of texts in which different dimensions of migrant workers' identities have been highlighted in the six newspapers.

Newspaper	Total texts	Texts highlighting political	Texts highlighting social and cultural	Texts highlighting economical
1.*People's Daily* (PD) (人民日报)	31	12	8	17
2.*Beijing Times* (BT) (京华时报)	45	9	11	30
3.*Jiefang Daily* (JD) (解放日报)	107	96	2	90
4.*Xinmin Evening News* (XEN) (新民晚报)	73	51	10	12
5.The *Southern Daily* (TSD) (南方日报)	5	3	0	2
6.*Southern Metropolis Daily* (SMD) (南方都市报)	17	4	8	5

Table 3.3. The highlighted dimensions of migrant workers' identity in the six newspapers.

The numeric summary of texts highlighting different dimensions of migrants' identities in each newspaper provides a general picture as to how the six newspapers portrayed migrant workers and which dimensions of their identities have been foregrounded. Irrespective of some possible overlapping or inconsistency in identifying identities of migrant workers due to the complexity of the milieu in which the text occurs, this table shows clearly that all the newspapers put a heavy weight on the political and economic dimensions of the migrant workers identities, describing them as an instrumental human source for economic development. Given the emphasis on their political and economic values in the media texts, the cultural and social roles of migrant workers, such as their roles as father, son, male or female, tend to be overlooked or disregarded in the media texts. From the analysis above, it can also be found that the migrant workers in China are very much framed as a political agency rather than as individuals with feelings, emotions and families, living everyday among the urbanites. This social group has been very much represented as social 'others' whose political or economic identities are the only ones valued and foregrounded in Chinese media discourse.

In portraying the migrant workers, these six newspapers differ in their choice of distinctive features. In the two Shanghai-based newspapers which unexpectedly possess the highest volume of coverage of this issue, migrant workers tend to be framed as low paid, low skilled, low educated workers, suffering from social insecurity. They are often exploited at work and owed withholding wages by employers. Drawing on Li's (2006, 2007) framework, these articles in the two Shanghai-based newspapers are packed with 'victim' plus 'negative behaviour' narratives and 'victim' plus 'being protected' narratives, with a very small proportion of articles describing their social and cultural roles.

Considering that Guangdong has probably hosted a larger proportion of migrant workers than any other province in China, the coverage of this issue by the two Guangzhou-based newspapers is very low in relation to its migrant population. Only 22 articles on this topic were found in these two newspapers. However, among these six newspapers, only *Southern Metropolis Daily* distinguishes itself from the others by presenting a rather different stance towards migrant workers. It publishes articles such as "Guangdong should still value the advantage of the inbound population" (Chinese: 广东仍旧应该珍视外来人口优势, 23 June, 2014, *Southern Metropolis Daily*), which treat immigrants from other places as an advantage to local development. In addition, this newspaper has the highest proportion of articles that highlight the social and cultural dimensions of migrant workers.

In terms of quantity of media articles, the two Beijing-based newspapers are situated in the middle between the Shanghai-based and the Guangzhou-based ones. The contents of their articles are inclined to be neutral, featuring governmental policies and efforts towards maintaining the social wellbeing of this social group, which includes providing medical and social insurance, social benefits and training to the migrant workers.

3.3.2. Key themes concerning migrant workers in the newspapers

In addition, the key themes covered in the six newspapers differ significantly, ranging from urbanisation to democratic election among migrant workers. Table 3.4 illustrates the key themes covered in the media texts of the six newspapers in 2014.

Key themes	***People's Daily*** **(31)**	***Beijing Times*** **(45)**	***Jiefang Daily*** **(107)**	***Xinmin Evening News*** **(73)**	***The Southern Daily*** **(5)**	***Southern Metropolis Daily*** **(17)**
Urbanization, employment	17	4	5	12	1	4
Medical and social insurance, social benefits, living conditions	11	0	4	21	1	4
Unpaid or with-holding wages, income	4	19	6	4	0	3
Stories of endeav-our	1	0	4	6	0	1
Spiritual civili-sation	3	1	0	0	1	0
Employment training	6	3	0	0	2	0
Returning to hometown	2	0	0	0	0	0
Nongmin Gong Children's Edu-cation	0	3	0	0	0	0
Victims of gang fight	0	2	0	0	0	0
The value of migrants	0	0	0	0	0	1
Democratic election	0	0	0	0	0	1
Others	0	0	88	30	0	3

Table 3.4. Key themes concerning migrant workers covered in the six newspapers.

The table above demonstrates that the themes covered in the six newspapers share a great deal of similarity, while possessing some distinctive differences. The key themes concerning migrant workers include discussions of the migrants' contributions to the process of urbanisation and their employment, their employment and living conditions, and the treatment of their unpaid or withholding wages. Other less-emphasized themes include their life stories and endeavour experiences in the cities. It is noted that in a large portion of the media texts under examination migrant workers are not the real central characters of the media coverage; instead the government or general public agencies which provide welfare and administrative support to this social group become the key protagonists in these texts. In other words, in these texts migrant workers are framed as inferior beings in the social hierarchy that need help and support from the upper and middle classes. This finding has reconfirmed previous research (e.g. Li 2006, 2007) that migrant workers are often framed as 'victims' or as 'being protected'. Moreover, the current study also finds that the media coverage does not foreground migrants' experiences and endeavours in the cities. That means the media articles seldom cover the story from the migrant workers' perspective, but mainly from the government's or the public agents' view. One typical example can be found in the following news text (Extract 3.1 here).

Extract 3.1

> 农民工市民化 财政得花多少钱
> 据国家行政学院测算，政府需新增支出1.8万亿元
> 2014-08-01 《南方日报》
>
> 7月30日，国务院出台《关于进一步推进户籍制度改革的意见》（以下简称《意见》），标志着户籍改革的大幕开启。同一天，国务院常务会议指出，部署做好为农民工服务工作，有序推进农业转移人口市民化。
>
> 户籍制度改革的"最后一只靴子"终于落地。落实户籍制度改革，还需要做好哪些配套工作，将给城市带来哪些变化？经济学专家认为，户改的关键还是推进基本公共服务均等化，而对中小城市而言，增加城市劳动力有利于扩大内需，提升城市经济的潜在增速。
>
> [How much would the Finance Department need to pay to make *Nongmin Gong* city residents?
>
> Chinese Academy of Governance estimates the Government needs new spending of 1.8 trillion *Yuan*
>
> *Southern Daily 2014–08-01*

On July 30, the State Council issued "Opinions on the further reform of the household registration system (hereinafter referred to as the Opinion)", indicating the commencement of the household registration reform. On the same day, the Executive Meeting of the State Council pointed out that the service work for migrant workers is to be deployed to transfer the agricultural population to city residents in an orderly fashion.

The "last boot" of the household registration system reform has finally landed. To implement the household registration system reform, what supportive work needs to be done? What changes will it bring about to the cities? The economists believe the key to such reform is to promote equal access to basic public services. As for the medium and small cities, the increase of city labour helps to expand domestic demand and enhance the city's potential growth rate.]

As shown in the above extract, the real focus of this article is to foreground the government decisions and actions re the household registration system reform, with the migrant workers being the patronised ones or the main recipients of these actions rather than the real key action performers. In grammatical terms, *Nongmin Gong* in these texts is always the object of the sentences, or the object of such words as "为"(for), "为了" (for), "把"(*ba*), "将"(*jiang*), "让"(*rang*) so they are always cast as the 'patient' (the recipients of the action) rather than the 'agents' (the performers of the action) in the sentences. Such media discourse conveys that the *Nongmin Gong* always take a passive role. This linguistic feature of portraying *Nongmin Gong* as the needy rather than the agents in the sentences can be widely found in most of the newspaper articles under examination in this book. In so doing, the journalists consciously or unconsciously frame migrant workers as persons upon whom the external agents, either governmental or non-governmental, should carry out actions. Such examples can be also be found in the following media texts. [Extract 3.2 here]

Extract 3.2

1) 为了让农民工兄弟姐妹吃好、住好，局里想方设法改善他们的生活条件，要求各环卫企业为农民工每天免费供应二荤一蔬一汤营养餐，高温期间还天天供应免费的牛肉粉丝汤、冬瓜骨头汤等营养汤。(1) (新民晚报, 2014-01-02) [In order to make migrant workers as brothers and sisters to eat well and live well, the bureau is trying to improve their living conditions by requiring sanitation companies to provide migrant workers every day with a free healthy meal with two kinds of meat, a vegetable and a soup, and during the high temperatures also to supply free beef vermicelli soup, pork bone soup with melon and other nutritious soups. (*Xinmin Evening News*, 2nd January 2014)]

2) 为帮助农民工成长、成才，近几年，区绿化市容局投入大量资金，输送他们到大专院校学文化、学技能。(1) (新民晚报, 2014-01-02,) [To help migrant workers improve and succeed, in recent years, the District Afforestation and Environmental Sanitation Administration invested heavily in sending them to colleges to study general knowledge and skills. (*Xinmin Evening News*, 2nd January 2014)]

3) 为了市民节前能搬进新居，并确保农民工按时返乡过年，各搬场公司提前包租大巴，既让农民工安心工作、为市民服务好，也免去了农民工排队购票的麻烦。(10) (新民晚报, 2014-01-29,) [In order to help the city residents move into their new homes before the New Year, and to ensure that migrant workers return home for the New Year's Day on time, every removal company arranged charter buses in advance to send migrant workers home. That enables migrant workers to work contentedly to serve the citizens, and it also removes from migrant workers the trouble of queuing up for the tickets. (*Xinmin Evening News*, 29th January 2014)]

4) 为农民工放映免费电影 (11) (新民晚报, 2014-01-29) [Free movies for migrant workers] [*Xinmin Evening News*, 29th January 2014)]

5) 在上海市安济医疗救助基金会的资助下，从2006年开始，浦东慈善医院组织"安济医疗志愿者服务队"，深入浦东新区各个工地，为农民工免费体检和义诊送药。迄今，已为浦东新区一百余个工地的两万多名民工进行了免费的全面体检。(39) (新民晚报, 2014-07-02) [Under the auspices of the Shanghai Anji Medical Assistance Foundation, starting in 2006, Pudong Charity Hospital has organised "Anji volunteer medical teams" since 2006 to go to each working site in the Pudong New Area. They deliver free medical check-ups and medicines to migrant workers. So far, they have provided free comprehensive medical examinations to more than twenty thousand migrant workers from 100 working sites in the Pudong New Area. (*Xinmin Evening News*, 29th January 2014)]

6) 为更好关爱农民工子女，减少暑期未成年人意外伤害事故的发生，复旦大学附属金山医院"大手牵小手"志愿者服务队的志愿者们近日来到金山石化五小，30余名外来务工子女接受了暑期安全教育。(42) (新民晚报, 2014-07-17) [In order to provide better care for children of migrant workers, reducing juvenile accidental injuries during summer vacations, Jinshan Hospital of Fudan University recently organized a "big hands holding little hands" volunteer service team. These volunteers went to Jinshan Shihua No.5 Primary School and more than

30 migrant workers' children received safety education in this summer vacation. (*Xinmin Evening News*, 17th July 2014)]

7) 让农民工坐飞机回家过年(61) (新民晚报, 2014-11-26) [Let migrant workers fly home for the New Year's Day holiday (*Xinmin Evening News*, 26th November 2014)]

With the intent of helping migrant workers, the media frame this disadvantaged social group as social 'inferiors' or 'victims' who need to be protected and educated. They have been often grouped as underprivileged citizens, together with unemployed, disabled and senior people. More examples can be found in the following extracts. [Extract 3.3 here]

Extract 3.3

1) 这些集中了老年、失业、残障、低保和外来农民工的"大居", 究竟该怎么管? （7）(新民晚报, 2014-01-16) [These 'big communities' are full of the aged, the unemployed, disabled, low income residents, and migrant workers. How on earth to manage them? (*Xinmin Evening News, 16th January 2014)*]

2) 中央文明办、中国志愿服务联合会发起"邻里守望"志愿服务活动倡议以来，嘉定区依托现有的志愿农民工服务网络，以空巢老人、农民工、残疾人、弱势群体为重点服务对象，围绕家政服务、文体活动、心理疏导、医疗保健、法律服务、救助帮困，建立起服务团队250多个、项目100多种，在册志愿者达8万多人。（37）(新民晚报, 2014-06-04) [Since the launch of the "Neighbourhood Watch" volunteer service campaign by the Central Civilisation Office and China Volunteer Service Association, Jiading District, which relies on the existing network of volunteers for migrant workers, it has provided services such as housekeeping, cultural and sports activities, psychological counselling, medical care, legal services, and assistance for the vulnerable. Their main target groups are elders staying at home alone, migrant workers, the disabled, and disadvantaged people. They have set up more than 250 service teams and over 100 service items with more than 80,000 volunteers registered. (*Xinmin Evening News, 4th June 2014)*]

3) 此次调查数据收集工作历时8个月，覆盖1800名网络用户，覆盖专业知识技术人员（如大学教授、律师、医生、记者、IT工程师等）、商界精英与高资产人士（如私营企业主、企业CEO等）、党政军体制内工作者（如公务员、军人等）和社会底层群体（如农民工、普通工人等）等。(62) (新民晚报, 2014-11-18)[The survey data collection lasted eight months, covering 1800 network users, including professional and technical personnel (such as university professors, lawyers, doctors, reporters, IT engineers, etc.), business leaders and high income individuals (such

as private entrepreneurs, enterprises CEO, etc.), workers within the military and political institutions (such as civil servants, military personnel, etc.) and underprivileged social groups (such as migrant workers, ordinary workers, etc.). (*Xinmin Evening News,* 18th November 2014)]

However, in some occasional cases, especially those published in *Southern Metropolitan Daily*, the life stories of migrant workers have been told from the migrants' perspective. Here below is just an extract [Extract 3.4] from a long story published on 2 February, 2014 in *Southern Metropolitan Daily* (see the original article in Appendix I).

Extract 3.4.

北宣恩土家族小伙李少国离家10年，从清洁工做到英语培训机构老板[Ten years' time since Shaoguo Li, a Tujia young man from the northern Xuan'en County, left his hometown saw him transiting from a cleaner to the owner of an English language training centre] 到年关就急着回家 一到家又牵挂工作 [So desperate to go home at the end of the year; so concerned about the work when at home] (南方都市报 *[Southern Metropolitan Daily]* 2014年2月2日 [2 February 2014])
Section subheadings of the article

- 李少国带着儿子回到老家。[Li Shaoguo brought his son back home]
- 打工第一年 穷得不敢回家过年 [The first year away from home, he was too poor to be back home for the Chinese New Year]
- 业余学英语 10年7次变轨 [Learning English in his spare time, he changed jobs 7 times during the 10 years]
- 想把英语培训学校开到家乡 [He wants to run an English training school in his hometown]

From the headlines and subheadings of the text above, we can recognize briefly the life trajectory of an ethnic minority man and his endeavour in the city. Living in the big city for 10 years, he is struggling between life in the city and his hometown, seeking to balance his identities between being a man from an ethnic minority village and being a businessman in the city. This life story was told using the third person single form 'he' as the subject of sentences throughout the article. Regardless of some other participants in the story such as his son, his parents, and his colleagues, Li Shaoguo and his life experience remain the key threads in this article.

Unfortunately, such stories from a migrant worker's perspective or having migrant workers as the real protagonists are not commonly found in contemporary Chinese media discourse. This suggests that China's media, especially the traditional print ones, are still heavily dominated by the authoritative ideology of their service as the mouthpiece of the party-state. In doing so, these media outlets still take the promotion of positive images of the party and the government as their essential mission. Despite the limited efforts put forward by some unconventional newspapers like the *Southern Metropolitan Daily*, which sometimes does investigate social issues in depth, the ideal of the media as a 'fourth estate' (Schultz 1998) is still much constrained by the government agencies and current social contexts. This issue will be further discussed in Chapter 6.

3.3.3. Text types of the media articles concerning migrant workers

This section examines the types of the texts concerning migrant workers published in these six newspapers. As discussed in Chapter 2, text types in this book refer to various rhetorical texts, such as media expository, media argumentative, media narrative and other hybrid types (see details in Chapter 2). Media expository explains what, how and why in the media text. Media argumentative is used to persuade that something is or should be the case or that something should be done. Media narrative tells stories about specific past events by following a temporal sequence. These text types might occur in a range of media genres, such as news stories, editorials, investigative reports, commentaries, etc. Below is a table summarising the primary findings concerning the primary text types found in each media text.

Newspaper	**Expository**	**Argumentative**	**Narrative**	**Hybrid**	**Total**
1.*People's Daily* (PD) (人民日报)	18	2	1	10	31
2.*Beijing Times* (BT) (京华时报)	21	4	0	20	45

Newspaper	Expository	Argumentative	Narrative	Hybrid	Total
3.*Jiefang Daily* (JD) (解放日报)	48	5	6	48	107
4.*Xinmin Evening News* (XEN) (新民晚报)	36	4	7	26	73
5.The *Southern Daily* (TSD) (南方日报)	5	0	0	0	5
6.*Southern Metropolis Daily* (SMD) (南方都市报)	6	8	2	1	17
TOTAL	134	23	16	105	278

Table 3.5. Text types in these six newspapers.

It can be seen in the table above that the predominant text type used to cover migrant workers in these six newspapers is 'expository'. About half of the articles under examination are expository. That concurs well with the dominant type of media discourse (i.e. news reports), used to provide information about current events. In this type of text, journalists present details of events often by following the typical news structure of an inverted pyramid with essential information at the beginning and more details at the end. By structuring the texts in this way, journalists cover "who is doing what to whom, when, where and how". In such media texts covering the migrant workers, 'who' is usually the government and its various agents, whereas migrant workers become the 'whom' that actions have been carried out on.

The second type of text identified is the 'argumentative' type that puts forward an idea/opinion with the support of reasoning and details. This type of text provides reasons to establish the truth or falsity of things. In media discourse, the argumentative type is usually seen in editorials or other opinion articles. For instance, in March 2014, *People's Daily* published an opinion article titled "The integration of *Nongmin Gong* (into cities) needs the power of local community" (Chinese: 农民工融入需要社区力量). In this article, the author argues that *Nongmin Gong* would assimilate more with the 'public nature of city residents', and the city residents would also change their views and attitudes towards *Nongmin Gong*, if they interacted and communicated more in local communities. It is assumed that this interaction and communication with local residents would accelerate *Nongmin Gong*'s integration into the cities. Although argumentative texts are not a big proportion of the articles under examination (23 out of 278), such texts do, or intend to, play an important role in guiding public opinion, especially those published by the mouthpieces of the party.

The third type of text is the 'narrative' that basically tells stories about migrant workers. Although only a small portion of the cohort (16 out of 278), these articles frequently portray how migrant workers' overcome difficulties in their endeavour to become successful and famous in their careers, or simply become rich. These kinds of 'success' stories have been framed as models for the migrant workers to change their ways and become independent from heavy reliance on external support. The successful migrant workers covered in these stories are from a wide range of social and geographical backgrounds, doing various jobs in the cities or in their hometowns usually after several years of city living experience. Such migrant life experiences have usually provided them with rich social insights and skills that are necessary for their ability to win through. This angle of framing the protagonists in the stories as successful persona also echoes well with the widespread societal ethos of being a success in Chinese society. Furthermore, these stories also feature the so-called "venturing or innovating" aspect (Chinese: 创业、创新) of the migrant workers. These stories usually depict how migrant workers find their own ways of developing their own businesses. The titles of the stories include "Small Chinese bamboo cats made a big article" (Chinese: 小竹鼠做出了大文章) (27/05/2014, *People's Daily*) and "Everyone's Chinese Dreams" (Chinese: "大家"的中国梦) (13/02/2014, *Jiefang Daily*). The publication of such stories is also driven by Premier LI Keqiang's advocacy of "National entrepreneurship and innovation" (Chinese: 全民创业、万众创新) in 2014 that encourages self-employment in running innovative businesses. Under the inspiration of the government, "national entrepreneurship and innovation" has become a mass movement widespread across China and has encouraged a large number of young people including migrant workers to find ways of being self-employed since 2014. This finding also reinforces the role of the media played in China as a mouthpiece of the party-state.

The fourth type of text identified in the data set is the ‘hybrid’ of different text types, predominantly the expository + narrative model. As a common text type in the various media, this expository + narrative model features exposition (expounding the key information) and narrative (conveying details to support the key themes). Another type of hybrid text is the argumentative + narrative model. Both models use narrative to support details for further articulation of the key statements in the texts.

3.4. Conclusion

This chapter first introduced the features of the six newspapers under examination and discussed the general trends in use of the terms *Nongmin Gong* and *Xin Shimin*/*Gongren* in the media discourse in China. Then, it examined the media representation of migrant workers in three aspects, namely, the identity dimensions, the themes, and the text types employed in the newspaper articles collected for examination in this book. This analysis finds that the six newspapers still predominantly used *Nongmin Gong* rather than the government-advocated *Xin Shimin* when discussing migrant workers. It is also noted that most newspaper articles foregrounded the political and economic identities of migrant workers, portraying them as an instrumental human source for economic development. Only a very few articles depicted the migrant workers as social and cultural agents, such as fathers, mothers, sons, daughters, and female or male community members living mundanely in cities with other dwellers. While they are frequently framed as victims or inferiors who need the protection, care, education, and welfare provided by governments and other public agencies, their social lives are rarely portrayed in these media texts. The themes covered in these newspapers highlighted the public protection and care provided to the migrant workers by the government and public organisations, and occupied a large proportion of the coverage. These themes include employment opportunities, medical care, social insurance, social welfare, employment training, and their children's education, etc. In most articles, the migrant workers were presented as the recipients of social actions and care, while the government and its agents played the roles of protector or carer of the migrant workers. It is contended here that framing migrant workers as protected or cared for might unconsciously reinforce the incongruous and unwelcome images of migrant workers that have long persisted in minds of the general public, especially many established city dwellers. This issue concerning the functions of media and media discourses will be further discussed in Chapter 6.

Regarding text types, the majority of the articles were found to employ exposition, argumentation, or hybrid type in which 'rational' or informative features predominate. The text type 'emotive' narrative (16 out of 278) that portrays the social or cultural dimensions of the migrant workers constitutes just a small portion of the data set. These findings concur with the identity dimensions findings in that only the political and economic aspects of migrant workers have been foregrounded. They also show that the social and cultural dimensions of migrant workers' identity are usually conveyed in narrative texts with migrant workers as the protagonists, whereas the political and economic dimensions of their identity are usually highlighted in expository and argumentative texts in which the government or public agencies are the key figures.

Another point worth noting in Chinese media practice is that journalists in China seldom focus on the migrant workers per se when covering their social mobility but mainly focus on the government agencies, public organisations, and industry sectors who can provide protection, care, and extra help to this social group. Few articles cover how the migrant workers, as living individuals, really work, live, and feel in the margin of society in this ever-changing era of China. These media practices will be further explored in the following chapters.

4. White-collar migrant workers in public media

The previous chapter examined the media representation of migrant workers in six influential newspapers in China, focusing on the highlighted dimensions of migrant workers' identity, the key themes covered, and the text types used in these media outputs. In light of the current developments of media discourse analysis which incorporate not only textual features but also media interactions and practices, the following chapter will turn its focus to examining the interactions between different media participants in constructing different images of and stances towards white-collar migrant workers in Chinese media discourse.

To that end, this chapter examines the social circulation (Spitulnik 1996) of two Chinese phrases *'he kafei'* (Chinese: 喝咖啡， i.e. drinking coffee) and *'18 nian fendou'* (Chinese: 18年奋斗， i.e. 18 years of endeavour) linked to white collar migrant workers in Chinese media discourse. These two phrases, identified as metapragmatic discourse (Silverstein 1976, 1993), employ the language of reflectivity to describe the life experience of migrant workers. The phrases have subsequently become objects of debate and public words encapsulating the inequality between migrant workers and established city dwellers in the media discourse. These two significant phrases and the debate around them initiated from a magazine article "我奋斗了18年才和你坐在一起喝咖啡"（I'm finally able to drink coffee together with you after 18 years of endeavour）originally published by *China Youth* (Issue 24, 2004), and republished by *Duzhe* in 2005 (see the article in Appendix II). This chapter will combine a sociocultural linguistic perspective on identity (Bucholtz and Hall 2005) and stance-taking theories (e.g. Bois 2007; Jaffe 2009) to examine how identities of and stances towards white-collar migrants have been constructed and mediated through a series of publications centred around these two phrases '*he kafei*' and *'18 nian de fendou*'.

4.1. Theoretical foundations

This chapter draws on a number of theories from western scholars in the field: the social circulation of media discourse (Spitulnik 1997), sociocultural linguistic construction of identity (Bucholtz and Hall 2005; Bucholtz 1999, 2002) and stance-taking (Bois 2007; Jaffe 2009). However, more importantly, for analysing Chinese discourses and communicative phenomena, Eastern paradigms of discourse studies (Shi-xu 2005, 2007, 2009) have been adopted to combine with the western-originated theories mentioned above with a view to taking a cultural, or multicultural, stance on discourse research. This includes a critical approach towards the western-originated theories to cater for the particularities and special features of discourses occurring in Chinese society. Indeed, it is imperative that Chinese cultural, intellectual and historical resources as well as the relevant principles in Eastern paradigms of discourse studies be drawn on to interpret the data collected and explore the communicative phenomenon in question. These theoretical frameworks pulled together from both the East and the West will provide the researcher with a repertoire of tools for conceptualising, analysing and interpreting the data.

A long-term goal in Shi-xu's academic agenda is the reconstruction of Eastern paradigms and/or the construction of Cultural Discourse Studies (CDS) in favour of multiculturalism in discourse research. According to Shi-xu (2005, 2007, 2009, 2010, 2012), one key principle for the construction and practice of CDS involves being locally grounded and globally minded with regard to culturally diverse perspectives and human concerns. In addition, he argues it is crucial to communicate with relevant international scholarly traditions in terms of concepts, theory, methods, especially those sharing similar concerns about the sociocultural contexts in which the discourses occur. Following this line, this chapter finds that both the sociocultural linguistic approach to identity and stance-taking share similar concerns with CDS in terms of sociocultural-specific needs and perspectives.

For the sociocultural linguistic analysis of identity as revealed by linguistic interaction, Bucholtz and Hall (2005) proposed a framework the key principle of which is that identity is the product rather than the source of linguistic and other semiotic practices. The sociocultural linguistic perspective on identity holds that identity is fundamentally a social and cultural phenomenon that emerges from linguistic and other semiotic practices. Identity in this framework is not simply viewed as a psychological mechanism of self-classification that is reflected in people's social behaviour but rather as something that is constituted through social action, and especially through language (Bucholtz and Hall 2005: 588).

Bucholtz and Hall (2005) also discuss and illustrate an important pair of concepts – adequation and distinction – in linguistic identity research. According to them, adequation emphasises the fact that in order to be positioned as alike, individuals or groups must be understood as sufficiently similar in any interaction which might index identity. In this kind of interaction, differences irrelevant or destructive to any efforts to adequate two people or groups will be played down. As the counterpart of adequation, distinction, originally conceptualised by Pierre Bourdieu (1984), is concerned with the production of social-class difference by members of the bourgeoisie. Bucholtz and Hall (2005) broaden its reference to include any process of social differentiation. Because language is an extremely important resource for producing social differentiation, the analysis of discourse or language used in this social process becomes a vital area of sociocultural linguistic research on identity.

Stance taking is perhaps the most important thing that people do with language. It, as defined by Bois (2007: 163), is "a public act by a social actor, achieved dialogically through overt communication means (language, gesture, and other symbolic forms), through which social actors simultaneously evaluate objects, position subjects (themselves and others), and align with other subjects, with respect to any salient dimension of the sociocultural field". In theorising and operationalizing stance analysis, this chapter will draw on the most well-known Bois' (2007) stance triangle (Figure 2.1), which is a geometric model that visually represents the interrelations between the three elements of stance-taking. Please see details in Chapter 2.

In analysing the social circulation of media discourse, we cannot avoid exploring the relations of intertextuality (following Bakhtin), which often feature some 'public words' that are recycled and recontextualised in succeeding communicative contexts. As argued by Spitulnik (1997: 161), when we examine communications emanating from the mass media, we see that, like most other forms of communication, they are preceded and succeeded by numerous other instances and pieces of language that 'both implicate them and render them interpretable'. The origin of these 'public words' (Spitulnik 1997) is sometimes, but not always, identifiable. They usually serve as a reference point or metapragmatic discourse, functioning metonymically to index the entire frame or meaning of the earlier text. The specific connotation that these words had in the original context drives their transportability into other communication events. Because metapragmatic discourse explicitly serves to frame and orchestrate communication, it tends to be more subject to awareness and segmentation than other linguistic forms (Silverstein 1976: 49). The general applicability of metapragmatic discourse is a significant feature that enables its recontextualisation in almost any kind of communication contexts.

4.2. The origin of *"he kafei" "18 nian fendou"* as a metapragmatic discourse

As mentioned above, debates around white collar migrant workers were initiated by an article named '我奋斗了18年才和你坐在一起喝咖啡'（I'm finally able to drink coffee together with you after 18 years of endeavour）originally published by *China Youth* (Issue 24, 2004) and republished by *Duzhe* in 2005 (see the original text in Appendix II). Both *China Youth* (中国青年) and *Duzhe* (读者, The Reader) are regarded as the top general interest magazines for the public in Chinese communities, especially, *Duzhe* which ranks third worldwide and first in Asia and China by circulation with an average monthly domestic and international circulation of over nine million. As a digest type of periodical, *Duzhe* publishes pieces of writing produced or recommended by its readers twice a month. High quality articles concerning the needs of the general public make

Duzhe an unparalleled print media source for research on Chinese people and society. As a result of *Duzhe*'s great influence on Chinese media and the general public, the republishing of this article in *Duzhe* has given rise to a huge amount of public interest and responses in both the print and Internet media in China.

In the article 'I'm finally able to drink coffee together with you after 18 years of endeavour', the author uses 'drinking coffee' metaphorically to refer to the urban or middle class life style. '18 years of endeavour' by the author alludes to the time for completion of a postgraduate education from primary school. The title of the article highlights the great efforts made by country-born migrants in their attempt to gain a similar social life to their counterparts in the metropolises. The article exposes the crucial facts of inequality between the city-born locals and the country-born migrants in terms of social values, ideologies, material powers, and social status. Eliciting numerous micro stories in demonstration of this inequality, this article has attracted enormous attention and provoked responses by people from every walk of life in Chinese society, especially those sharing similar life experiences.

Since publication of this article, the two phrases 'drinking coffee' and '18 years of endeavour' have become a metapragmatic discourse (Spitulnik 1997) which has been recycled in various communicative contexts discussing the social inequality between the two groups. As demonstrated in Spitulnik's (1997) chapter of radio phrases, which have been recycled from the realm of radio into contexts of face-to-face communication in Zambia, metapragmatic discourse is not the only kind of discourse which is transported across communicative contexts, but it is readily seized upon due to its particular kind of transparency of both form and function (Silverstein 1993). In the current chapter, *China Youth* and *Duzhe* as China's leading general interest magazines, together with other media in China, have lent prominence to the two phrases under discussion and fuelled the prevalence and repeatability of these phrases, through association with colourful identities or stances and heightened drama of the migrant workers.

4.3. Identity of migrant workers constructed around these two phrases

In describing and representing the identities of white collar migrant workers, the author of the original article adopted a radical "I" versus "you" rhetoric, which would be regarded as a 'distinction' strategy (Bucholtz and Hall 2005) in linguistic identity research. This rhetoric dominates the text with 'I' referring to the country-born migrant workers and 'you', the city-born counterparts. All micro stories or anecdotes involve the pronouns "I" or "you", forming sharp contrasts in numerous social aspects between these two social groups. This strong 'I' versus 'you' rhetoric differentiates these two social groups, making the 'I' group, i.e. the group of country-born workers, stand apart from its city peers. It is evident that this distinction between "I" versus "you" was deliberately employed to highlight the clefts between two social groups, which tends to be perpetuated by the Chinese social order and system.

Here is, for example, an extract from an original text by *Maizi* (2004).

Extract 4.1 (from the original text):

> 从我出生的一刻起，我的身份就与你有了天壤之别，因为我只能报农村户口，而你是城市户口。如果我长大以后一直保持农村户口，那么我就无法在城市中找到一份正式工作，无法享受养老保险、医疗保险。你可能会问我："为什么非要到城市来？农村不很好吗？ 空气新鲜，又不像城市这么拥挤。"可是农村没有好的医疗条件，去年SARS好像让大家一夜之间发现农村的医疗保健体系竟然如此落后，物质供应也不丰富，因为农民挣的钱少，贵一点儿的东西就买不起，所以商贩也不会进太多货。春节联欢晚会的小品中买得起等离子彩电的农民毕竟是个别现象，绝大多数农民还在为基本的生存而奋斗，于是我要进城，要通过自己的奋斗获得你生下来就拥有的大城市户口。[From the moment of my birth, my identity and yours have a great gap, because I can only be on a rural *hukou* (household registration system), and you have been on a city one. If I remain on a rural *hukou* I won't find an official working position in the city, will be unable to enjoy the old-age pension and medical insurance when I grow up. You might ask me: "why cities? Isn't it good in rural areas? There is fresh air, unlike the city, so crowded. "But there are no good healthcare facilities in rural areas. SARS last year makes you aware overnight that the rural health care system is so backward without sufficient material supply. As farmers earn less money, there are little things they just can't afford, so traders don't keep much in stock.

The farmers in the Spring Festival TV Gala Show, who can afford plasma TV, after all, are isolated cases. The vast majority of farmers are still struggling for basic survival, and so I want to go to the city, by my own efforts, to gain a city *hukou* which you attained at birth.]

This extract illustrates how the *hukou* would incur different social statuses and social welfare, potentially inciting social inequality. This *hukou* system is widely regarded as a source of unfairness, but there is also fear that its liberalization would lead to massive movement of people into the cities, causing strain to city government services, damage to the rural economies, and increase in social unrest and crime. Though controversies about this system have been around for years, the system is still dominant in the social life of Chinese people. But the story doesn't dwell on the issue of *hukou*, which has been discussed and debated extensively. It moves on to discuss the pathway for a rural resident to gain an urban *hukou* through seeking employment in cities after university. In line with his/her life encounters, the author shares the experiences of inequality in education, university admission, tuition fees, and daily life. Though feeling ill-treated in this process, the author still feels satisfied and pleased that s/he is able to 'drink coffee' with his/her city counterparts after 18 years of endeavour.

Another feature concerning the identities of white collar migrants is that the authors tend to be self-denigratory and self-effacing in construction of an identity that is inferior to their city-born counterparts. This feature, originating in traditional Chinese culture, has been perpetuated in contemporary Chinese society and it bears deep social significance. This feature of self-denigration and self-effacement can be exemplified in the following extract.

Extract 4. 2 (from the original text)：

来到上海这个大都市，我发现与我的同学相比我真是土得掉渣。我不会作画，不会演奏乐器，不认识港台明星，没看过武侠小说，不认得MP3，不知道什么是walkman，为了弄明白营销管理课上讲的"仓储式超市"的概念，我在"麦德隆"好奇地看了一天，我从来没见过如此丰富的商品。[Upon my arrival in the metropolis of Shanghai, I found that I was the ignorant country boy in comparison with my classmates. I'm unable to paint, unable to play a musical instrument, do not recognise Taiwan and Hong Kong pop stars, have not read Kung Fu novels, do not know the MP3, and I do

> not know what is a Walkman. In order to sort out the concept of "warehouse supermarket" taught in the marketing management course, I was wandering in "*Maidelong* supermarket" curiously for a whole day. I have never seen so much merchandise before.]

In this extract, the author purposely presents himself as clueless and uneducated in comparison with his city-born counterparts. But the subtext here might be that although "I" was so 'stupid and uncivilised' before, I have achieved comparable social status with you after my 18 years of endeavour or simply outperformed 'you' in many ways. In this sense, 'my' self-esteem has been greatly enhanced. As Cai et al. (2011) observe, being modest can boost self-esteem, this makes sense when put into the context of a culture that places a premium on fitting in with others. It is perceived that when Chinese behave in a modest way, they view themselves higher or feel better deep inside their hearts (Cai et al. 2011). This might result from the collectivist characteristics of East Asian cultures, especially China. Self-denigration for the purpose of self-enhancement may appear contradictory to Western societies. However, "Chinese would partake in the cultural drama by deemphasizing the positivity of the self at an explicit level when high on modesty or when situationally induced to behave modestly; however, they would paradoxically benefit from their modest disposition or situationally induced behaviour by implicitly harvesting an enhanced self" (Cai et al. 2011: 62). In the case under discussion, the author purposely denigrates himself/herself with a view to emphasising the gaps between "I" – the country-born – and 'you' – the city born and highlights the 18 years of endeavour so as to yield an assiduous and striving self-image.

4.4. Data collection

To investigate the inequality between these two social groups and the popularity of these two phrases, a Google search of the two phrases 18年奋斗 (18 years of endeavour) and 喝咖啡 (drinking coffee) was carried out in Chinese websites for three time periods from 2004 to 2012. Here below are the findings of this search.

Range of time period from 2004 to 2012	Search instances
01/01/2004 to 31/12/2006	About 94,000
01/01/2007 to 31/12/2009	About 811,000
01/01/2010 to 17/07/2012	About 2,830,000
	Total: About 3,180,000

Table 4.1. Internet search for the two key phrases.

This table demonstrates that more than three million instances of these two phrases were found on the internet from 2004 to 2012, while the recent three years (2010 to 2012) witnessed a sharp increase in public concern about social inequality between the two social groups. It appears that this sharp increase in public concern might partially be attributed to the publication of this debate.

With the aim of examining the social circulation of the media discourses around the two phrases '*kafei*' and '*18 nian fendou*' as well as the stances derived from them, some data were selected from the large cohort for detailed analysis in accordance with the following criteria. First, only articles that directly responded to the original article and were concerned with the white collar migrant workers in China were collected; second, the articles had generally to be over 300 Chinese characters to provide enough space for the writers to build up arguments and simultaneously to exclude microblogs and short blog posts, which take up a large proportion of the over three million instances; third and most importantly, only articles with titles including either of these two phrases or their variants were collected. This ensures that an 'intertextual series' (Hanks 1986) is formed among the selected articles which index a set of stances that align or dis-align with the original author. In other words, data collection was aimed at including all substantial articles with clear arguments and stances closely responding to the two phrases in question and the issue of social inequality experienced by the migrant workers. In addition, high selectiveness of data makes the data size manageable with a focus on the perceived inequality experienced by the migrant workers.

In the data collection process, it was found that the majority of the over three million instances on the Google list were simply duplicates of the original article in different print media and websites, especially in discussion forums and blogs, where articles such as this usually provoke large numbers of short comments. Most of these comments only indicate whether the respondent agrees or disagrees with the original view expressed in the text in a limited number of words and with little cogent argument and justification. This observation will be further discussed in relation to the analysis of stances in the following sections.

Searching within the timeframe of seven years, the data collection was narrowed to cases of stance-taking which responded not to a prior stance in the immediate context, but to prior stances displayed in a series of articles from general interest magazines, newspapers, and websites in China. As a result, 15 articles or blog entries published in the period of 2005 to 2012 fulfilled all criteria and were selected for detailed analysis in this chapter.

Stancetaker	**Title /Publication source issue/year**	**Author**
Insiders		
1 我奋斗了18年才和你坐在一起喝咖啡 [I'm finally able to drink coffee together with you after 18 years of endeavour] *(Original text)* *China Youth* (中国青年), Issue 24, 2004; (Republished) *Duzhe* (读者), Issue 8, 2005		麦子 *Maizi*
2 我奋斗了18年不是为了和你一起喝咖啡 [My 18 years of endeavour are not for drinking coffee with you] *China Youth-China Youth* Daily, (中国青年报）24 July 2007		优游 Youyou
3 我奋斗了十八年就是为了和你坐在一起喝咖啡 [My 18 years of endeavour is just aiming to drink coffee with you] http://www.duwenzhang.com 文章阅读网 2012		水木刀 shuimudao

Stancetaker	Title /Publication source issue/year	Author
Insiders		
4 我奋斗了18年，却来不及和你坐在一起喝咖啡[I've endeav-oured 18 years, but there's no time for me to drink coffee with you] http://www.shu0.net/?p=10864 树洞网 2010		树洞 shudong
5 我奋斗了18年，也不能和你坐在一起喝咖啡 [I've endeav-oured 18 years, but still cannot drink coffee with you] http://www.duanwenxue.com 短文学网 2011		柚子茶 youzicha
6 另一篇：反驳-我奋斗了18年才和你坐在一起喝咖啡[Another one: Refute – I'm finally able to drink coffee together with you after 18 years of endeavour] http://www.douban.com 豆瓣网2011		七月风 qiyufeng
7 读后感 --《我奋斗了18年才和你坐在一起喝咖啡》 [A reader's response to " I'm finally able to drink coffee together with you after 18 years of endeavour"] http://blog.csdn.net/crcr/article/details/6632863		计算机人生 Computer life
Public intellectuals		
8 奋斗了18年，咖啡还能喝多久 [Upon 18 year endeavour, how long can you enjoy the coffee] 中青在线 (www.cyol.net) November 2010		王石川 Wang Shichuan
9 "阶层固化"日趋严峻：奋斗18年 咖啡能喝多久 ["Social class entrenchment" getting fortified: how long can you drink coffee after 18-year struggling] *China Youth Daily*, (中国青年报） 16 November 2010		
10 "我奋斗了十八年才和你坐在一起喝咖啡"的时代还存在吗 [Is there a time for 'I'm finally able to drink coffee together with you after 18 years of endeavour'? *http://book.douban.com* 豆瓣网		柏拉A梦 Bola A Dream

Stancetaker	Title /Publication source issue/year	Author
Public intellectuals		
11 《我奋斗了18年才和你坐在一起喝咖啡》读后感 ['I'm finally able to drink coffee together with you after 18 years of endeavor' A reader's response] *http://www.1666666.net/duhougan27/*		admin
12 阶层固化现状：农村娃奋斗18年能和城里人喝咖啡 [The state of class entrenchment: Country boys can drink coffee with city boys after 18-year endeavour] http://gongyi.people.com.cn/GB/13235895.html 人民网		
Common outsiders		
13 其实，不喝咖啡又如何 [In fact, what about no coffee] 新浪博客(www.blog.sina.cn) March, 2011		程云芬 Cheng Yunfeng
14 十八年后喝上咖啡又怎样 [Then what about drinking coffee after 18 years] 中国经济网 经济博客 http://blog.ce.cn/		水晶首饰 Crystal jewellery
15 喝了咖啡又如何[After drinking coffee, then what] 中国国土资源作家网 http://www.gtzyzj.com		admin

Table 4.2. Examples of responses to the two phrases.

The above Google search and the examples of responses have shown that the two phrases have been circulating widely both in China's institutionalised (e.g. public owned newspapers and magazines) and personalised media (e.g. blogs and websites for youth). The authors of the articles selected have deployed these two phrases as a metapragmatic discourse, on one hand, to contextualise their own articles into the debate circle; on the other hand, to claim their own space of self-expression and stance toward the issue in question through variation of these phrases. Through these two phrases and their variants, an 'intertextual series' has been formed to highlight the interrelatedness between the original text and other texts. As Coupland (2007:114) observed, "authors often quote or reconstruct the words of other people, and in doing so they can inflect those sources' voices in various ways, giving them particular identity traits and qualities".

These fifteen articles represent divergent stances towards the migrant workers and the social inequality they experienced. In accordance with the author's identity shown in the text, the articles are categorised into three stance groups, namely, insiders, public intellectuals, and common outsiders. The first seven articles represent insiders' stances in which the authors identify themselves with the original author as being from a similar background of countryside or remote inland places. The second group of authors are public intellectuals who usually take a scholarly approach to the issue of migrant workers. The third group who are named common outsiders don't consider themselves as members of either the migrant workers or public elites. But, they provide comments on this issue on the basis of their own viewpoints and personal experience. These three groups of texts provide an interesting intertextual series in representing and interpreting a previously understated social wrong (Fairclough 2012) in Chinese society.

4.5. Stance-taking

To analyse the stances taken by the different groups of authors, Bois' stance triangle is adapted to explore the complexity of interaction between the object (i.e. the issue under discussion) and the subjects (i.e. the authors from different social groups). In view of the aim of the original framework to analyse oral communication in an immediate context, the current chapter deals with a communicative or interactive event on a much larger scale in terms of participants, time range, and spatial distance. In other words, this framework is applied to the analysis of a communicative/interactive event discussing a social issue with a large number of participants over a wide range of time and spatial distance through institutionalised and personalised media. That means that the participants in this investigation (i.e. authors of the texts) engage in intersubjectivity at a greater temporal distance. But, as argued by Bois (2007), the only element crucial to the construction of intersubjectivity is orientation to a 'shared stance object';

that is, when multiple authors evaluate the same stance object, they are aligning themselves with respect to each other.

4.5.1. Insiders' stances

The authors in this group feature a commonality of identifying themselves as white collar migrant workers. They emphasise similarities with the original author in experiencing inequality in various social aspects. That is they employ adequation (Bucholtz and Hall 2005) to index their identity as migrant workers. However, their stances towards the inequality differ greatly, especially in terms of whether to set up their life goal to '*he kafei*' (drink coffee) or not. The original author's 'after 18-year endeavour I am able to drink coffee with you' indicates a positive attitude towards the social status that they can achieve. Several authors in this group present an opposite stance towards this issue and disapprove of the original author setting a life goal as '*he kafei*'. Especially, Author 2, with a negatively changed title (我奋斗了18年不是为了和你一起喝咖啡 [My 18 years of endeavour are not for drinking coffee with you]), takes up a stance opposite to Author 1's viewpoints.

Extract 4. 3 (from Text 2):

> 3年前，麦子的一篇《我奋斗了18年才和你坐在一起喝咖啡》引起多少共鸣，一个农家子弟经过18年的奋斗，才取得和大都会里的同龄人平起平坐的权利，一代人的真实写照。然而，3年过去，我恍然发觉，他言之过早。18年又如何？再丰盛的年华叠加，我仍不能和你坐在一起喝咖啡。 [3 years ago, *Maizi*'s "I'm finally able to drink coffee together with you after 18 years of endeavour" caused much resonance. A farmer's child, upon 18 years of endeavour, could only have won equal rights with their counterparts in mega-cities. It is a true picture of this generation. However, 3 years have passed by, and I have come to recognise that it's too early to come to the conclusion. How about another 18 years? No matter how many years have been added up, I still cannot sit with you for coffee.]

In this extract, Author 2 evaluates the stance of Author 1 by stating 'it is a true picture of the generation'. However, while taking the same 'you' vs. 'I' rhetoric and positioning him/herself as a country-born white collar migrant, Author 2 goes against Author 1's stance and argues that it is too early to come to the conclusion that the country-born would achieve a similar social status to their city-born counterparts after 18 years of endeavour. Author 2 contends that the gaps between these two social groups are still much larger than imagined and it is not possible for them to sit together for coffee, no matter how many years 'I' endeavour.

In this group of articles, a clear opposition to the original author's positive view has been formed to argue it is not possible to drink coffee with the city-born counterparts upon 18 years of endeavour. However, some authors, for example, in Text 3, still follow the arguments of Text 1, insisting that the common right of 'drinking coffee' with the city-borns is their life goal no matter how hard the endeavours would be. It shows their determination to achieve equal rights after years of hard work. However, some others (Texts 4 and 5) fall into a pessimistic stance that demonstrates the helplessness and despair that they experienced after years of struggling in the marginalised life. On the other side of the debate, some authors stress the importance of attitudes toward life. They stress that though it's hard for their generation to 'drink coffee' with their city-born counterparts, their endeavour to be independent and courageous would be the personality traits they pass on to their descendants. In the face of the daunting topic of human equality and social justice, some authors opt to dodge direct treatment of this topic and take perceptions and attitudes towards life as a way to counterbalance the gaps between these two social groups.

It is also noted that most authors in this group employ an emotional tone in incorporating their personal stories and anecdotes to align with a positive or negative stance toward the issue concerned. The commonly used genre could be regarded as a kind of narrative + exposition which illustrates their viewpoints by examples of their personal stories.

4.5.2. Public intellectuals' stances

This group of authors usually adopts a scholarly approach to the issue by employing a genre of exposition rather than the narration with anecdotes found in the previous group. By referring to and evaluating the original text 1, the author of Text 8 acknowledges at the start the impact that the original text had on the public. Then, the author draws on social theories and terms (e.g. social class entrenchment, social class downgrading) to analyse the social factors behind the gaps.

Extract 4. 4 (from Text 8)

> 多年前，一篇名为《我奋斗了18年才和你坐在一起喝咖啡》的网文，吹皱了亿万网民的心潮。…… 是的，知识改变命运，奋斗成就人生……多年来，这样的励志名言鼓舞了无数贫家子弟不断与命运抗争，然而，如今，这样的成功史似乎越来越像传奇了，取而代之的是阶层固化。[Many years ago, an article titled 'I'm finally able to drink coffee together with you after 18 years of endeavour' stirred up a tidal surge of emotion of millions of Internet users. … Yes, knowledge changes destiny and endeavour accomplishes life … For many years, countless poverty-stricken youths have been inspired by such mottos to keep struggling against fate. However, today, such stories of success seem increasingly like a legend. It is replaced by social class entrenchment.]

With evidence from research conducted by the Chinese Academy of Social Sciences, this author points out that 'now the opportunities to become a cadre for students from cadres' families are 2.1 times higher than those from non-cadres families' and 'the ratio of students from a country-born background at Peking University has reduced from 70% in 1950s to 16.3% at present'. In an effort to reveal the depressing reality by employing social theories and research findings, the author aims to caution the public that 'upon 18 years of endeavour, how long will you be able to enjoy the coffee'. 'You' might have to go back home to the countryside to drink 'water', due to social class entrenchment and social class downgrading.

The authors in this group generally take a similar scholarly approach by using theories and social research findings to analyse and explain the issue of concern.

4.5.3. Outsiders' stances

Text 13 is an article written by a so-called 'middle-aged housewife', who evaluated several relevant texts in the first paragraphs of her article. This author argues that too much emphasis has been given to materialistic satisfaction in our current era. As she put it, a well-balanced pursuit of both material and spiritual life should be upheld.

Extract 4. 5 (from Text 13)

> 功利时代的到来，并不意味着可以忽略内心的需要。但是，即便是内心的需要，匆忙，也并不可取。不论你是什么样的事业，我们都要给我们的心灵保留一个开阔的空间，一种内在的从容和悠闲。过去的六年，我感悟很多很多，不再固执一定要最好，不再刻意攀比。　当然，物质年代，保留一些限度之内的追求，但不至于迷失，让生活对我们也保留适当的诱惑，不至于被这个时代淘汰得太远，亦也不失为一种从容的生活方式。[The coming of a utilitarian age does not mean you can ignore the inner needs. However, even if it is what the heart needs, haste is also not desirable. Regardless of what kind of business you are in, we have to keep open space in our minds, an inner tranquillity and light-heartedness. In the past six years, there is a lot that I have come to recognize: no longer stubbornly craving for the best; no longer deliberately comparing with others. Of course, in this materialistic age, we should retain a number of pursuits within limits, but not to get lost in them. To maintain appropriate temptations in life, and not to be left too far behind by this age, it will be a relaxed lifestyle.]

By positioning herself as someone outside the 'I' and 'you' groups in the previous texts, this author represents an outsider's stance in dealing with the issue concerned. What she advocates could be regarded as a well-balanced life style in pursuit of both material and spiritual satisfaction. The author believes that an unbiased stance would be the resolution to the issue under consideration. That is, 'what about no coffee' in search of a healthy lifestyle, in which deliberate comparison with others should be avoided. Authors 14 and 15 in this group also accentuate whether never to drink coffee really matters. The elegance of life does not depend on where 'you sit, the utensils you use, or the price you pay for coffee. It depends on the attitude that you take towards life'.

4.6. Conclusion

Following Bourdieu (1992, 2002 [1977]), it is assumed that communication is fundamentally about the pursuit of symbolic power and that cultural capital achieved through language is simultaneously material, social, and economic. In engaging in intersubjectivity at a greater temporal distance, the fifteen authors examined in this chapter construct an interactive process in China's media by addressing an issue of common interest. This interactive process, on the one hand, demonstrates that mass communication in contemporary China has witnessed a thorough change in making forums available for people to express their divergent stances towards issues of concern; on the other, a seemingly overt 'social wrong' (Fairclough 2012) can be addressed and reflected by people from different social backgrounds with divergent perspectives, using language resources (e.g. genre, vocabulary, rhetorical devices) with a view to gaining symbolic power (Bourdieu 1992, 2002) for one disadvantaged social group – the migrant workers in China. This might be progressive evidence of Chinese society marching into a more open-minded and rational civilisation.

This chapter analysed the linguistic manifestations of taking divergent stances in both the print and Internet media in China. These differentiated stances can be argued as specific instances of what Hodge and Kress (1993) refer to as the production of social difference in texts. Drawing on the concepts of dialogism, heteroglossia, and intertextuality, Hodge and Kress argue that all text production relies on past or current, recognisable or imperceptible contributions by co-present or absent authors and takes place within social structures characterised by the unequal distribution of powers. The production of different texts reinforces these structures, and social actors are then assumed and trained to adopt unequal positions of power in particular types of texts and interactions. As revealed in the chapter, the authors deal with the same social issue using different genres, linguistic devices, and social attitudes. While the authors in the insiders group emotionally articulate the social inequalities between the country-born and the city-born in social life with an enormous amount of micro-stories and anecdotes, the authors in the public intellectuals group analyse the issue with research findings and scientific data in a typical scholarly genre of exposition. The authors categorised as common outsiders express their opinions with an attempt to re-orientate the debate to the pursuit of a more spiritual life rather than material satisfaction. It is hoped that this analytical finding has strengthened Hodge and Kress's argument that the production of different texts reinforces the social structures, characterised by the unequal distribution of social powers.

In addition, although this chapter demonstrates that public forums are now available for common people in China to articulate their viewpoints and stances towards a social issue through a range of public outlets, the quantity and quality of the opinions and the stances expressed in this chapter are still very limited. It can be argued that the variety and complexity of public opinions and channels available to express public views are important indicators of a civilised society. Even though over 3 million instances concerning the two phrases were identified in this chapter, it appears that only a small amount of these established rigorous arguments with clear indications of independent thinking and convincing justification. This suggests that there might still be a long way to go before the diversity and sophistication of opinions and stances concerning public issues can be formed and articulated in China's media.

Theoretically, this chapter has provided a demonstration that a discourse research project should always be 'locally grounded and globally minded, historically conscious and contemporarily helpful' (Shi-xu 2009:41). In analysing discourses occurring in such a high-context language as Chinese, it would be insufficient to simply apply western-originated theories to the structural or functional analysis of texts per se. Rather, the valued philosophical ideas, concepts, theories, and methods of Chinese cultural-intellectual heritages must be drawn on to supplement the Western-originated theories and methods, especially those with deep concerns about culture-specific needs, such as sociocultural or ethnographic approaches to discourse (e.g. Blommaert 2005; Bucholtz and Hall 2005; De Fina and Georgakopoulou 2012; Jaffe 2009; Rampton 2006). Approaches and methods drawn from both East and West together provide an optimal repertoire of frameworks and analytical tools to analyse Chinese discourse and communication phenomena in greater depth.

5. Construction of migrant workers' identities on a TV talk show

The previous two chapters examined the representation of migrant workers by the print and Internet media in China, addressing such questions as how the key newspapers represent migrant workers and how authors from diverse social backgrounds construct different identities of and stances towards white-collar migrant workers in Chinese media discourse. This chapter will turn its focus from print and Internet media to television media, which still occupies a vital position in the mass media in China.

5.1. Introduction

This chapter examines how identities of migrant workers (i.e. *Nongmin Gong*) have been constructed and represented on a TV program in China. The primary data for this chapter come from two different streams: one is the TV talk show program, broadcast by the Guizhou Satellite TV (GZSTV) in China; the other consists of interviews and observation notes taken during a 10 day fieldwork in 2012 in which the researcher interviewed the program staff members and observed their production process. With its boastful name 'China's *Nongmin Gong*' (Chinese: 中国农民工) and its position as the first of its kind in TV talk shows, this TV program has achieved great success, winning many top prizes for TV programs, such as the national prestigious 'News Prize in China' and the 'Star Prize' for Chinese popular TV programs.

Guizhou Satellite TV (GZSTV) is a provincial broadcasting system based in south-western China, Guizhou province. Located in the inland and being one of the undeveloped areas of China, this province has become a major exporter of *Nongmin Gong* to other parts of the country every year. According to the 2006 census, there are 4.5 million *Nongmin Gong* from Guizhou's 39 million population, working in different parts of China. This provides the GZSTV with an enormous number of cases and inevitable responsibilities to report on this floating population. Moreover, GZSTV claims to have beamed to over 700 million audiences all across the country with a wide range of programs broadcast through its one satellite channel and nine local channels.

This 'China's *Nongmin Gong*' program was first launched in 2007 in the context of widespread commercialisation and entertainmentisation of mass media in China. With a view to promoting the public image and recognition of this special floating population, the TV program features 'true life stories' of *Nongmin Gong* using a tone that appeals to its targeted audience. As pointed out by the then CEO of GZSTV (Bai 2008), the success of this program lies in the authenticity of the stories and the respectful attitude taken towards this social group on the program. As a main stream state-run media institution, GZSTV launched the *"China's Nongmin Gong"* program with the aim of establishing 'a communication platform' between people from diversified backgrounds against a backdrop of massive social change in China. In the world today, there is a high demand for people from different socio-economic backgrounds to have access to physical and virtual platforms to articulate their voices and exchange ideas in hopes of enhancing understanding of those lacking reciprocal trust and respect (Bai 2008). As a social group stigmatised with derogatory status and viewed as lesser identities by some urbanites, *Nongmin Gong* have striven to earn social recognition and respect along with negotiating and modifying their identities to cater for their changing life.

Drawing on discourse and sociolinguistic theories concerning narrative and identity, this chapter will examine identities of the migrant workers co-constructed and represented on this TV talk show. In discourse studies, sociolinguistics and anthropology, narrative or storytelling is considered the 'basic', most 'essential', mode of human communication. It is experience-as-told and as made social (Blommaert 2005:84). As argued by Lorenzo-Dus (2009: 40–41), the stories told in TV programs can fulfil a number of mutually inclusive functions, such as the articulating of debate, the display of lay experience as a counterbalance to expert systems of knowledge, the construction of a sense of intimacy conducive to the public baring of participants souls, and more importantly here, the creation of the impression that certain aspects of the socio-historical world are being directly addressed. Thanks to the designated social goals of this TV program, the migrant workers represented on this program demonstrate personality traits of being positive about life and of striving to succeed in their transition to urban life. In such a process, the TV program tends to transform the entrenched perspective of *Nongmin Gong*'s abnormal identities to normality and even to highlight its supernormality in the program. One focus of this chapter is to examine the supernormality of *Nongmin Gong*'s identities represented in the program with a view to elucidating the identity struggle that the migrant workers have experienced in their transition from rural to urban.

In this talk show program, storytelling/narrative is the key means through which particular aspects of reality and specific facets of the interviewees' (i.e. *Nongmin Gong*) identities are co-constructed between themselves and the program host. By virtue of being selected to participate in the talk show, the interviewees are recognised as outstanding or supernormal migrants, asked to share their life stories in the context of massive internal migration in China. However, they despite being lay participants in TV programs, they are expected to tell 'true stories' about themselves and deliver 'authentic talks' in expressing their opinions. Consequently, their participation in the program is very much controlled or even manipulated by the program directors, editors or more importantly by the program host in the studio, all of whom hold a mission to realise the social functions of the TV program. Thus, the other focus of this chapter lies in examining the discursive practices that the program is drawing on in this sociolinguistic co-construction of migrant workers' identities. In particular, it analyses the discursive practices of the media employed at three distinctive stages, namely 'off stage', 'back stage', and 'front stage' in this sociolinguistic co-construction process of the *Nongmin Gong*'s identities, in the process of which the interviewees' personal experiences are transformed into TV programs to appeal to the public audience.

This chapter is divided into two sections. The first looks at the supernormal identities of the migrant workers represented in their personal-experience stories and examines key facets of the migrants' personal stories selected by the media. The second section explores how the migrant workers' personal-experience stories are transformed to public narratives. It focuses on analysing discursive strategies adopted by the media, especially by the program host, to construct particular individual and social identities of migrant workers to be contextually appropriate.

5.2. From abnormality, normality, to supernormality

In light of the contemporary public discourse of abnormality (Dong 2013) around migrant workers in China, the TV program under examination foregrounds some key dimensions of migrant workers' identity in the hope of counter-balancing the prevalent public discourse. The notion of abnormality, attributed to Michel Foucault's *Abnormal* (2003), is used in Dong's research (2013) on language and migrant identity, in which she argues that the migrants are often regarded as 'abnormal individuals'. According to Dong (2013), this is partly due to the fact that migrants are unable to be integrated into the normative system, but also due to their tendency to introduce disorder and disruption to the normative system. According to Foucault (2003:162), the norm is the rule of conduct, the tacit law, the principle of order and conformity, against which irregularity, disorder, disorganisation, dysfunction, deviation are measured and disqualified. In this sense, Dong (2013) argues that contemporary public discourse in China often regards migrant workers as persons that deviate from 'normal' and who are to be corrected.

Regarding the public discourse of abnormality around *Nongmin Gong*, the TV show program 'China's *Nongmin Gong*' can be viewed as serving as a counter-discourse (Foucault 1977) to the imposition of abnormality on their identities and as advocating a normality or even supernormality on them. Foucault contends that every social discourse which involves a politically generated truth-claim encounters a counter-discourse that challenges the original discourse's legitimacy. In this case, what the program aims to do is to demonstrate to its audiences that the *Nongmin Gong* are 'normal' the same as all other urbanites and are even 'supernormal' under the lens of the program. To be selected as part of the program, the *Nongmin Gong*s on the show have to demonstrate personal traits that greatly exceed the normal or average in their peers. The advocacy of 'normal to supernormal' identities by the media will be further examined in the following section.

The data examined in this chapter include three seasons of the 'China's *Nongmin Gong*' program consisting of 48 episodes broadcast across 2007–2009. With one season each year, the data cover around fifty interviewees telling their life stories on the TV screen to the general public. The stories feature personal endeavours such as winning success in big cities, fighting for their children's rights to get public education in cities, upholding rights in pay negotiation, etc. The piecemeal life stories told by the interviewees form a larger-than-life portrayal of the public images of this distinctive social group in the urbanisation process in China. Blum-Kulka (1997) points out that TV talk show programs tend to use exceptionality as the main criterion to assess lay participants' entitlement to enter the program, even though they are invited to the program precisely because of their being ordinary people. In this case, the unexceptional tellers' exceptional tales favoured by the 'China' *Nongmin Gong*' program depict a commonly seen social group with unusual life experiences and stories.

Although the *Nongmin Gong* life experiences presented in the program differ greatly in their details, they have some personality traits in common which might have made these particular interviewees seem exceptional and thus stand out from their peers. As a result, their normality or supernormality is foregrounded in the TV talk show programs.

5.2.1. Diligence, frugality, and striving for success

The most prevalent features of the stories of the *Nongmin Gong* on this program are diligence, frugality and striving for success. Extract 5.1 offers a typical example of the emphasis on these locally relevant personality traits. The setting is a story about a brother and a sister working in Guangdong to make money for their impoverished family in

Guizhou. Here, Yu Dajiao (the sister) presents herself as someone capable, hardworking and frugal in providing support to her poverty- and misfortune-stricken family. When she first arrived in the small town in Guangdong, she displayed a proactive disposition, volunteering to work overtime, taking tests for employment, prudently saving money, etc. Then, after showing her conscientiousness and honesty at work (L. 4), she got promotion from an ordinary worker and became an inspector. Her life changes due to her own efforts and so does her family life back in Guizhou.

Extract 5.1

> 广东东莞市青溪镇 -- 地处广州与香港经济走廊的中间。这里云集了七百多家外资企业，三十多万来自全国各地的打工者，在这个小镇上，寻找着各自不同的梦想，余大娇是这只寻梦大军中的一个。因为态度好、能力强，还常常主动要求加班，她的工资在宿舍是最高的，而她的花费却是所有女孩子当中最少的，在消费不低的青溪镇上，她每一个月只用一百来块钱。身边的姐妹们逛街买化妆品、买新衣服，余大娇从来不掺和，她甚至尽量避免和她们一起出门。(Qingxi town, Dongguan, Guangdong is located in the middle of the economic corridor between Guangzhou and Hong Kong. Here more than 700 foreign-funded enterprises employ more than 300,000 migrant workers from around the country looking for their dream in this small town. Yu Dajiao is one of those hunting their dream here. Due to her good attitude, ability, and willingness to volunteer to work overtime, her salary is the highest in a dorm, but her spending is the lowest among all the girls. In the context of high costs in Qingxi, she only spends around 100 *Yuan* every month. Girls are often shopping around to buy cosmetics and new clothes. Yu Dajiao never mixes with them and even avoids going out with them altogether.)

1) 主持人 / 你干的是什么工作? (Interviewer/What kind of work do you do?)
2) 余大娇 / 我现在干的是检查员。(Yu Dajiao/I'm now working as an inspector.)
3) 主持人 / 是一个技术性比较高的工作嘛! (Interviewer/ It is a technical job now!)
4) 余大娇 / 对。开始因为在里面做事认真、老实，最开始是(普通)员工，最后提到检查员，因为检查员是较好的一个部门。(Yu Dajiao/ Ye. Because I started working with conscientiousness and honesty. At the beginning, I'm a (normal) employee, and was promoted to be an inspector because inspectors are in a good department.)
5) 主持人 / 这个工作是招进去的，还是考进去的? (Interviewer/ You got the job through recruitment or a test?)

6) 余大娇 / 凭自己的实力考进去的，那个厂的效益也是比较好。(Yu Dajiao/ Through test by my own strength. The salary in the factory is relatively good.)

In this episode, she (Yu Dajiao) also presents an unusual facet of her identity – courage and confidence (L. 4 and L.6) – in answering the interviewer's questions regarding what kind of job she is doing and how she got this job. These two aspects of identity are not commonly seen in a young girl of her age (early 20s) and from a similar background; they are usually shy and nervous in their public presence. However, it shows in the extract that Dajiao believes in her self-efforts and strengths which have brought her success at work and in life. The manifestation of her courage and confidence might be the reason that she was chosen to be one of the participants in the program.

5.2.2. Perseverance and confidence in life

Another common feature of the interviewees' identities represented in the program is perseverance and confidence in the face of difficulties. Due to their usually disadvantaged background, *Nongmin Gong* frequently encounter diverse challenges in their migration life. Without a determined and tough mind, they can very easily end up as nobodies in the city. The following extract is a typical story about a successful migrant worker.

Extract 5.2

> 1977年邓启茂出生在娄山关脚下——— 一个叫九龙的小山村，因为家庭贫困，16岁那年他第一次走出家门，来到浙江温州，开始辗转打工的生涯。他在湖南、广西修铁路；在广东东莞的建筑工地，做水磨石地板；在浙江温州养猪、扫马路，在街头扮演米老鼠；在广东中山当仓库管理员，从普通打工仔，到身兼多职的打工皇帝。邓启茂历经7年打工之路后，终于在2001年创办了——这家属于自己的工厂。(Deng Qimao was born in 1977 at the foot of Mt. Loushanguan – a little mountain village called Jiulong. As his family was poor, he left home at the age of 16 for the first time, and went to Wenzhou in Zhejiang Province, starting his career as a *Nongmin Gong* for everywhere. He worked for railway construction in Hunan and Guangxi; worked on terrazzo floors at a construction site in Dongguan, Guangdong; raised pigs, swept roads, played Mickey Mouse in the street in

Wenzhou, Zhejiang; worked as a warehouse administrator in Zhongshan, Guangdong province. From an ordinary wage-earner, to a multi-experienced superior worker, in 2001 Deng Qimao founded his own factory after 7 years as *Nongmin Gong*.)

1) 邓启茂 / 2005年的时候，生意非常火爆的时候，动不动一年随便赚200多万的，那个时候我的厂又太小了，2000多个平方，厂房不行了，得搬。然后一搬工厂就特别不顺．被盗。…… 我记得那天早上，我们厂车间有人打电话："哇!不得了!"我说怎么了?他说模具被偷了!我说偷多少? 他说差不多偷完了。那一瞬间我真的有点，站不起来的感觉。心想特别的……完了!完了! (Deng Qimao/in 2005, when business was very hot, it was just easy to earn more than 2 million a year. At that time my factory was too small, with no more than 2000 square meters. It had to move. And the factory was stolen… I remember that morning when someone from our factory workshop called "wow! " I say what's up? He said the mould was stolen! I asked how much was stolen. He said almost all. For a moment, I was really kind of, unable to stand straight. Especially felt … … it's over! Over!)
2) 主持人 / 有没有想过干脆算了，那么多事，这企业办起来也太累，太难了!干脆不办了，算了? (Interviewer/Ever thought of giving up? That's so much, and also too tired to run an enterprise, too difficult! Simply forget about that?)
3) 邓启茂 / 那不可能，我这么多年辛辛苦苦创下的基业，没有可能让它付诸东流，没可能，绝对不可能!…… 我从小不算命，我相信命运是靠自己双手把握的。(Deng Qimao/No way, I've worked hard to set a legacy, not possible to get wasted, no way, absolutely no way! … … I never see a fortune teller. I believe that your fate is grasped in your own hands.)

This extract offers an unusual story about Deng Qimao, who started working as a penniless *Nongmin Gong* in many parts of China and finally became the boss of his own factory in Guangdong. No matter what difficulties or problems he encountered, his tough and optimistic personality let him believe that his fate should be in his own hands. Before discussing the nature of this identity, it is necessary to remember the double articulations of broadcast talk, which is locally triggered yet designed and produced for audiences situated elsewhere. In his performed true-to-experience talk, he presents himself as someone who has undergone numerous sufferings (i.e. discrimination, misunderstanding, contempt, robbery, financial crisis, etc.). Yet he survived and prospered later in his life using his wits, and relying on his tough and optimistic personality. These aspects of identity seem to be the important factors that lie behind the success stories of the interviewed *Nongmin Gong* in the program.

5.2.3. Action with visions and strategies

While diligence and perseverance are the features of the *Nongmin Gong*'s identities often depicted and highlighted in the program, many episodes in the talk show also suggest to its audience that taking actions with vision and strategy is another important aspect of identity that helps the *Nongmin Gong* succeed in their endeavour to resettle in a new place. Extract 5.3 shows Qiang Xinggui, a *Nongmin Gong* from Guizhou, running a telephone Hotline for his peer migrants in Cixi, Zhejiang Province. To provide psychological support and community services to his peer migrants struggling to settle in an unfamiliar place, he chose to resign from management positions in big enterprises and run a telephone Hotline for his peer migrant workers in Cixi, where it turned out to be a good business (i.e. the telephone Hotline). His vision to life is evidenced by his action of setting up this service and his strategy to seek support from the Harmony Association and the local government. In *Nongmin Gong*'s endeavours to achieve a better life in cities, the visions and strategies they adopt most probably determine the positions they are able to achieve and the life they can have. Just working hard on a routine track without a clear goal would surely lead them to nowhere. Diligence is a desirable aspect of identity that this TV program advocates, but working with an unambiguous goal and vision is another crucial facet of identity that this TV program encourages *Nongmin Gong* to possess.

Extract 5.3

> 墙兴贵当年只身来到慈溪，先后在多家企业打工，担当过很多企业的管理工作职务。墙兴贵最初只是考虑自己如何融入慈溪这个大环境，而现在他更多的是考虑如何帮助大量外来务工青年，与慈溪人一道共同建设和谐的社会环境。2006年，当陈家村成立和谐促进会时，他当上了副秘书长，并且开办了外来务工人员排忧解难的热线电话。而他的各种努力，也得到了人们的承认，2007年，他在宁波383万外来务工入员中，

被评为"十大感动宁波的外来务工人员"。(Qiang Xinggui came to Cixi alone that year. Working in a number of enterprises, he served in the management of many businesses. Qiang Xinggui initially only considered his own integration into the environment in Cixi, but now he is considering how to help a large number of migrant youth build together a harmonious social environment in Cixi. In 2006, he became a Deputy-Secretary-General of the Harmony Association which was founded in Chenjiacun Village, where he also opened up a Hotline for the migrant workers. All his efforts were acknowledged by the people. In 2007, he was placed in the "Top Ten Migrant Workers in Ningbo", among the 3.83 million migrants in Ningbo.)

1) 主持人/墙兴贵啊，你在开办"小墙热线"之前，你在做什么？(Interviewer/ Qiang Xinggui, what did you do before you ran the 'Xiao Qiang Hotline'?)
2) 墙兴贵 / 当时我是在工厂里面管生产。(Qiang Xinggui/ I was in charge of manufacturing in a factory.)
3) 主持人 / 你的收入还挺不错的。(Interviewer/ Your income should be pretty good.)
4) 墙兴贵 / 当时的收入，加上年终奖的话，每年在十万左右。(Qiang Xinggui/ Income at that time, including the year-end bonus, was around 100,000.)
5) 主持人 / 那你办这个"小墙热线"，是你自己办的，自己掏钱办的? (Interviewer/ Then, why did you run this 'Xiao Qiang Hotline' with money from your own pocket?)
6) 墙兴贵 / 当时是我自己办的，最后成了整个慈溪市和谐促进会的"小墙热线"。(Qiang Xinggui/It was run by myself at first, but later it became the 'Xiao Qiang Hotline' of the whole city and the Harmony Association.)
7) 主持人 / 你怎么会想到要办"小墙热线"呢? (Interviewer/ Why did you want to run the 'Xiao Qiang Hotline'?)
8) 墙兴贵 / 办"小墙热线"的目的就是说，第一点，让当地企业相信我们贵州人确确实实在改变，确确实实改变好了，让更多的企业老总相信我们贵州人，接纳我们贵州人。(Qiang Xinggui/ The purpose of running the Hotline, first, is to let the local enterprises believe that Guizhou people are really changing, really changing for the better, and to let more CEOs believe in our Guizhou people and accept our Guizhou people.)

As a marginalised or disadvantaged social group in Chinese society, *Nongmin Gong* are usually distant from the mainstream city culture and barely able to enjoy the social welfare of their urban counterparts. They are the most vulnerable spectrum of society in the face of natural disasters and economic turbulence. Thus, how to survive well is a big challenge for the *Nongmin Gong* without appropriate *hukou* (household registration) status while providing the cheap labour needed for the country. It could be argued that the facets of identities being foregrounded in the talk show program, such as diligence, frugality, perseverance, sagacity, and more importantly, success in life, stem from both the traditional and the contemporary Chinese ethos. While Chinese people are widely acknowledged as a hardworking population, to become successful in life has become a prevalent tenet in contemporary Chinese society. Everyone aspires to succeed in whatever they do for life in that society regardless of the nature and the true meaning of success. It is widely apparent that books, articles, talks, seminars on how to become successful pervade every corner of society. This talk show program, as one media operating in this context, inevitably draws on this ethos in its selection of interviewees and promotion of the desirable identities of *Nongmin Gong*.

This program chooses to interview the *Nongmin Gong* with the purpose of providing this disadvantaged social group with encouragement and inspiration through modelling of the interviewees' personal life stories. In the process of developing this program, the program crew work together to transform the personal experience of the participants into a public narrative which contributes to the construction of the exceptional identities of the *Nongmin Gong* that the media aims to create. The exceptionality in their identities pinpointed by the media attempts to construct the normality or supernormality of *Nongmin Gong*'s identities in the audience's perception. The next section explores how these identities have been co-constructed by the media and the participatory *Nongmin Gong* themselves.

5.3. Co-construction of the identities

This section discusses the discursive practices that the media adopts in constructing the identities of *Nongmin Gong* in the 'China's *Nongmin Gong*' program. This analysis will highlight the discursive strategies that the TV program crew, especially the interviewer, employ in this sociolinguistic co-construction of the identities of *Nongmin Gong* in the program. The analysis of this process will be unfolded with a demarcation of three phases of *Nongmin Gong*'s performance, i.e. off stage, back stage and front stage. Drawing on a dramaturgical model of social interaction analysis, social interaction is analysed in terms of how people live their lives as actors performing on a stage (Macionis and Gerber 2011). This model has its origin in Goffman's work (1956), which made an important distinction between 'front stage' and 'back stage' behaviours. As the term implies, 'front stage' actions are visible to the audience and are part of the theatrical performance. People engage in "back stage" behaviour when no audience is present. This analytical model offers a look at the concepts of status and role of the interaction participants. Status refers to a rank or a position that one holds in a group, or a society, while a role is like a part in a play, such as father, mother, son, and worker. Status might also refer to the honour or prestige attached to one's position in society. In frame analysis, Goffman (1974: 298) writes, "What is important is the sense he provides them through his dealing with them of what sort of person he is behind the role he is in". The dramaturgical perspective posits that the individual's identity is performed through role(s), and consensus between the actor and the audience. Goffman also described each individual's "performance" as the presentation of self, a person's efforts to create specific impressions in the minds of others. This process is sometimes called "impression management". Another important term that will be employed in this study is 'off stage' which refers to situations relating to the participants' private life, which is usually invisible to the audience and where the individuals can perform themselves and drop their social roles and identities.

In this specific program about China's *Nongmin Gong*, the TV program crew make a careful choice about which potential *Nongmin Gong* participants would be eligible to join the program and share his/her stories with the audience. The pre-production interview and direction of the 'lay' interviewees aims to make sure that the participants' front-stage performance meets the requirements of the program. As the most crucial means employed by the media to construct the identities of *Nongmin Gong*, selectivity is applied to the acquisition of potential interviewees, the life stories underpinning their identities, and their subsequent dissemination to the public. Selectivity, as a universal feature of producing any media, is exercised at every stage of this program production. The program crew attempt to choose the most favourable subjects (interviewees and their life stories) and perspectives to report them with a view to fulfilling the social purpose of the program.

In the TV program under discussion, the lay participants hold the status of *Nongmin Gong* and play the roles of interviewees in their interactions with the interviewer. Prior to the live talk show, the interviewees' 'off stage' life has been invaded and interfered with by the program crew, who have visited them and shot video clips of their private realm. Then, the interviewees are placed 'back stage' to get prepared for the 'front stage' show, facing the audience on site and those in front of the TV screens. Thus, there is a clear distinction between the 'off stage', 'back stage' and the 'front stage' in this sociolinguistic construction of identities, so exploring what really happens 'off stage' and 'back stage' prior to the analysis of the 'front stage' co-construction of their identities might be worthwhile.

Consequently, the key research question addressed in the following section is how the *Nongmin Gong*'s personal life experience has been transformed into public narrative by the media. In other words, what discursive practices have been employed by the media to co-construct the identities of *Nongmin Gong*? The analyses will follow the three separate stages mentioned above.

5.3.1. Reaching into the 'off stage' life

Upon being spotted by the media, the interviewees' 'off stage' life is invaded and interfered with by the program crew, who usually pay an on-site visit to the potential interviewees. In this on-site visit, the crew observes, records and interacts with the interviewees and the people around them. Short video clips are shot to focus on some facets of the interviewees' life experience that are considered 'useful' for the program.

At this stage, the interviewees are briefed about the goals and procedures of the TV program. Thus, the *Nongmin Gong*'s 'off stage' life and space, which was previously invisible to the audience, has been accessed by the crew and aspects of their life are captured for the TV presentation.

5.3.2. 'Back stage' preparation

In the 'back stage' of the program preparation, the interviewees are invited to the studio for setting up the 'front stage' performance. Despite it being claimed a live show, this program makes the participants fully aware of what they should talk about on the show and how they should do it. As a crucial step of the 'back stage', the producer and the program host have a 'lengthy talk' with the interviewee to decide what will be covered at the 'front stage'. The 'lengthy talk', so called by the program director, usually takes several sessions over a few days, enabling the program crew to have a thorough understanding of the participants' life, and, more importantly, enabling them to draft a script for the live show on the basis of this 'back stage' interaction.

This script (see extract in Table 5.1), which serves as a running sheet for the program, covers the key steps of the program and the major points that the program host will bring up. As the professional presenter, the host controls the shape, the length and even the content of the program by following the running sheet with its key questions and points. Below is an extract of such a running sheet with the pre-scripted host's key questions.

序号 (no.)	**环节 (steps)**	**内容 (content)**	**要点(key tips)**
1	开 场 (opening)	(key lines by the interviewer) 观众朋友，这里是"中国农民工"讲述节目，欢迎收看。欢迎我们节目的嘉宾，来自北京的孙恒，也欢迎来参加我们节目的现场的观众朋友们。先来看一个短片来认识一下今天做客我们节目的嘉宾。 (Dear audience, here is the "China's Migrant Workers" program, welcome. Welcome Sun Heng, the participant from Beijing to our program. Also welcome the audience to the site to participate in our program. First, a short film to introduce our guest for our program today.)	
…	…	…….	

序号 (no.)	环节 (steps)	内容 (content)	要点(key tips)
4	Video clip 2	(Introduction to the school run by Sun Heng) 同心实验学校位于北京朝阳区的金盏乡皮村，距市中心有近两小时的车程。孙恒选择在这里办学校，一是因为地价便宜，二是因为这里聚居着众多的外来打工者，而本地村民只有外来人口的十分之一。(Tongxin Experimental School is located in Pi Village, Jinzhan Township of Chaoyang District, Beijing, about two hours' drive from the city centre. Sun Heng chose here as the location for the school; first because land price is cheap, second it is inhabited by a large number of migrant workers; local villagers constitute only one-tenth.) ……	
5	演播室访谈(studio interview)	(key questions by the interviewer) 1. 问：孙恒有没有孩子？他的孩子将来会不会在这里读书。(Q: Does Sun Heng have children? Will his children attend school here?) 2. 打工学校的创办是因为孙恒和他的团队意识到将来他们这些打工者的孩子没地方就读所以就要办一所学校(The migrant workers school was founded because Sun Heng and his team realized that these migrant kids have no school to attend.) 3. 他们每次都是遇到问题 去解决的过程中寻找到新的途径(They always have problems to solve in the process of finding new ways.) 4. 在为农民工唱歌的过程中他们成立了打工青年艺术团，孙恒担任团长(For singing to migrant workers, the working youth ensemble was established, and Sun Heng served as the head.) 5. 问：你怎么想到成立打工青年艺术团的？(Q: How did you think of the establishment of the working youth ensemble?)	突出那段打工经历给他带来的人生影响(Highlight the impacts that work experience made on his life) 这个阶段还处于寻找人生道路的迷茫时期(This stage in his life is the lost time in finding out his life goal.)

Table 5.1. A sample of the running sheets for the program

5.3.3. 'Front stage' performance

The 'reality' talk show interweaves two main sites of the participants: the immediate site of the studio, in which the interview takes place, and the visually marked and dynamic sites from the interviewees' daily life, which have been captured by the pre-recorded video clips. As indicated in Table 5.1, the interviewee in this episode was a music teacher at a rural primary school before migrating to Beijing to become a singer. In Beijing he also ran a school for children from migrant families. At the beginning of the program, the host introduces him with a pre-recorded video clip, presenting his background and his school for migrant children. Using the pre-scripted opening remarks and key questions, the host facilitates direct access to the socio-historical world from which the interviewee comes to tell viewers 'true stories' about 'real people'.

As the key player in the reproduction of the *Nongmin Gong*'s life stories, the program host acts as a coaxer who helps the lay participants spell out what the media wants them to say, encouraging them to dwell on certain aspects of their stories and telling the stories in a particular tone of voice. These practices can be simply termed scaffolding in co-construction of the desirable identities of *Nongmin Gong* for this program. Scaffolding practices include strategies of eliciting, positive feedback, reinforcement, bridging, and, more importantly, foregrounding and backgrounding of specific aspects of the participants' identities. These discursive strategies are discussed below.

5.3.3.1. Eliciting and positive feedback

Eliciting and positive feedback, commonly employed by the host to introduce the stories or topics, are often manifested in the form of a question, or a statement as a reminder in the live interview.

Extract 5.4

1) 主持人 / <u>你干的是什么工作?</u> (Interviewer/What kind of work do you do?)
2) 余大娇 / 我现在干的是检查员。(Yu Dajiao/I'm now working as an inspector.)

3) 主持人 / 是一个技术性比较高的工作嘛! (Interviewer/ It is a technical job now!)
4) 余大娇 / 对。开始因为在里面做事认真、老实，最开始是(普通)员工，最后提到检查员，因为检查员是较好的一个部门。(Yu Dajiao/ Ye. Because I started working with conscientiousness and honesty. At the beginning, I'm a (normal) employee, and was promoted to be an inspector because inspectors are in a good department.)
5) 主持人 / 这个工作是招进去的，还是考进去的? (Interviewer/ You got the job through recruitment or exam?)
6) 余大娇 / 凭自己的实力考进去的，那个厂的效益也是比较好。(Yu Dajiao/ Through an exam with my own strength. The salary in the factory is relatively good.)

In this extract, the host deliberately forms the questions about the interviewee's current job by following the eliciting strategy step by step. First (L.1) is the opening question to start the topic; second (L.3) is the elaboration of the topic and positive feedback to what she has done; third (L. 5) is an alternative question (i.e. you got the job through recruitment or a test), exploring how the interviewee got the job. This eliciting strategy aims to highlight two key points regarding the interviewee: 1) the interviewee got a technical job with a higher status due to her '认真、老实' (conscientiousness and honesty); 2) she got the job via passing an exam due to her own capacity. This eliciting strategy enables the host to introduce the topics and guide the interviewees through to spell out the desirable stories.

5.3.3.2. Reinforcement and bridging

Reinforcement, a strategy used to confirm and stress the interviewees' remarks and feelings, is frequently observed in the host's front stage performance. For instance, in the story about Yu Dajiao (details in Ext 5.1), the following questions (see Ext. 5.5) are found in the host's utterances. Note that the questions here are for emphasis or to seek confirmation of the previous remarks rather than to elicit different answers from the interviewee. Here the host purposely repeats or strengthens the interviewees' utterances to draw the attention of the audience.

Extract 5.5

1) 余大娇 / 一件衣服才十五块。(Yu Dajiao/It is just 15 *Yuan* for each piece of clothing)
2) 主持人 / 十五块钱啊!?(Host/ Only 15 *Yuan*?!)
3) 余海深 / 开始的话，我一般都是买一下衣服。买的衣服都是很便宜，都是在三四十块钱以下的，都是很便宜的，然后就没有其他的了。(Yu Haishen/ At the beginning, I started with buying some clothes. All the clothing are very cheap, below 30–40 *Yuan*, very cheap, then, buy nothing else.)
4) 主持人 / 就没有其他的了?(host/ Nothing else?)

Another strategy employed by the host is 'bridging' which is used to change topics and keep up the pace of the program. The host uses hedge phrases or structures, such as 'it seems…', 'I heard that…', 'it is heard that…' to move from one topic to another when she needs the interviewee to get onto it immediately. For instance,

Extract 5.6

1) 主持人 / 好像你当时思想斗争挺利害的，好像还专门请了一天假去看了一下上海?(Host/ It seems that at that time you were quite conflicted and asked one day leave to visit Shanghai.)
2) 主持人 / 你在那儿，刚开始去的时候，也干的是装卸工，后来听说你当队长是自荐的，自己推荐自己的? (Host/ You were a loader as the start there. Then, it was heard that you self-recommended yourself to be the team leader, self-recommended?)

Here the host uses phrases or sentences to introduce a new topic that she wants the interviewees to talk about next. It is a strategy commonly used by the host to control the pace of the program and to help the interviewees cover the anticipated stories that the program requires them to spell out. It is assumed that in the 'back stage', the host has acquired all the stories that will be told 'on stage'. He is just using this bridging strategy to prompt the new topic to be covered in the onstage performance on time.

5.3.3.3. Foregrounding and backgrounding

Drawn from Fairclough's work on discourse and social change (1993), foregrounding refers to the practice of emphasizing some concepts or issues in the text, while backgrounding alludes to the practice of playing down concepts or issues in the text. The term 'foregrounding' would overlap in some cases with the term 'reinforcement' and be similar to 'positive feedback'. Backgrounding is probably more implicitly presented than foregrounding in this program. However, a distinctive example found in the data set is in the life story of a migrant worker called Deng Qimao (Extract 5.7).

Extract 5. 7

1) 邓启茂 / 之后就犯了一点小小的错误。(Deng Qimao/ Then I made a little mistake.)
2) 主持人 / 什么错误?你能不能跟我们说一说? (Hostess/What's wrong? Can you tell us about that?)
3) 邓启茂 / 进入那个厂，每天都吃夜宵，每个人就用那个煮粥，煮完粥之后都有菜吃，我还不知道这个菜从哪里来的。但是有一天突然有人告诉我，今天晚上轮到你俩了，我就问干啥啊?那人就讲了，弄菜去. 可能就是偷菜了。当时就比较胆怯，不愿意去。但是人家说你了，我们天天弄给你吃，你吃了我们. 你不去弄不行啊，去的过程当中就被逮着了。(Deng Qimao/In the plant, we eat midnight snack every day. Everybody has the congee. After the congee, there is usually vegies. I don't know where this came from. But suddenly one day, I was told, tonight it's your turn. I asked what? The man spoke, to get the vegies. That might be stealing. Cowardly, not willing to go. But they spoke to me. We gave you every day, and you eat ours. You have to go, but I got caught in the process.
4) 主持人 / <u>等于就是到农民的菜地去摘点菜? (Hostess/ It</u> appears that you <u>pick some vegetables</u> from the farmers' farm?)
5) 邓启茂 / 到菜地我还没有去摘，我就在路边站着看他摘。他去摘，来人了，他跑了，把我逮着了。……(Deng Qimao/I haven't picked, but standing on the sidewalk I saw him pick. He picked and the people came. He ran away, and they caught me. …)
6) 主持人 / <u>等于第一次出门就遇到了很不顺心的事情? (Hostess/ In the first time out, you met something very unpleasant?)</u>

Here the host attempts to background the interviewee's misconduct of stealing by calling it 'pick vegies from the farm'. While misconduct such as stealing and violence has been a common complaint by the urbanites against *Nongmin Gong*, the host here deliberately downplays this complaint in order to promote positive images of this population.

Note that the hostess does not condemn the *Nongmin Gong* for this conduct, just mentioning it as something unpleasant in his first time away from home. It appears that the hostess, given the purpose of the program, decides the talk show is not the right place to deplore the misconduct.

5.4. Discussion and Conclusion

As a result of the pre-arranged manipulation and co-construction employed by the media in representing the identities of *Nongmin Gong*, the program has attracted an audience who presumably enjoy the stories, feel sympathy with the migrants, and empathize with the migrants' life experience and perceptions. Through these interpenetrations of the public and privates spheres, the private life experiences of the interviewed *Nongmin Gong* are transformed into public narrative. It is argued that the program under examination serves as a counter-discourse to challenge the legitimacy of the public discourse of abnormality around *Nongmin Gong* and advocates the normality or supernormality of the floating population via three distinctive stages of manipulation and co-construction.

In this sociolinguistic co-construction of *Nongmin Gong*'s identity, the context, 'space' and 'place', and the purpose of the program very much shapes the participants' performance of their identities. Though all the narratives are based on their life experiences, the way that the stories are told and the points being highlighted depends greatly on the manipulation of the program host and other crew members. Their presentation of 'diligence, frugality, confidence, and action with vision' in the interviewed *Nongmin Gong*'s identities could be regarded as a shaped supernormality represented for the purpose of the program. As observed by Blommaert (2005: 224), people can (and do) shift places 'frequently and delicately, and each time, in very minimal ways, express different identities'. So in this sense, the identities that *Nongmin Gong* establish on this TV talk show, in some cases, may be separate and different from their 'offstage' identities. It could be suggested that the identities presented on TV are just the desirable facets of *Nongmin Gong*'s identities that the program selects to present to its audience in order to fulfil the social function of the program.

The above chapter also revealed that the TV crew drew on diverse linguistic resources to transform personal experiences to a form suitable for public discourse. As a demonstration of the sociocultural linguistic approach to discourse analysis, it is to be noted that this small-scale study drew on a wide range of theories and concepts, including sociocultural linguistic theories in identity and interaction, the dramaturgical model of social interaction, Foucault's 'abnormality', Fairclough's 'foregrounding and backgrounding', just to name a few. This fusion of theories and concepts constructed a theoretical repertoire to address the research question of the study, i.e. how the identities of migrant workers have been constructed and represented in the public media in China. Employing both ethnographic and linguistic methods, this chapter exemplifies the modern interdisciplinary trend to explore social issues (i.e. the public media practice in China in this book) through examination of language use by using the sociolinguistic approach to discourse.

6. Media representation and practice in Chinese contexts

It took much longer than I expected to write up this monograph investigating the representation of migrant workers in Chinese media. On the long journey of examining how their identities and stances have been constructed and mediated through media discourse in Chinese contexts, this book, to a great extent, has followed the developmental trajectory of discourse analysis as a research discipline that has transited from a text-focused orientation to a more practice and process focused direction. Along the way, a diverse range of theoretical frameworks and data sources have been drawn on, and their significances and consequences will be considered in this concluding chapter. I would like to start this discussion by summing up the key analytical findings in the previous three data based chapters.

Being the first data analytical chapter in this book, Chapter 3 focussed on how the migrant workers have been represented in the influential newspapers. Following a text-focused approach, the analysis covered the foregrounded dimensions of identity, the key themes selected, and the most commonly used genres in the media coverage of migrant workers. The findings revealed that only the political and economic dimensions of the migrant workers' identity have been brought to the fore in the six influential newspapers in China newspapers. In their media representation by the key newspapers, the migrant workers are less framed as normal city dwellers than as political and economic human resources contributing to the economic development of the country. Their personal lives and experiences seem to be of little interest to the media, instead, most media articles highlight the government or public agencies as the protagonists who provide care and protection to these underprivileged migrant populations. The newspaper articles show that the public protection and care provided to the migrant workers by the government and public organisations are the real focuses of the media. This might be deeply related to the social function of the public media in China which is to be the mouthpiece upholding the party and the government, a task more vital than reporting on the common public.

This chapter also reported that most media articles employ exposition, argumentation, or some hybrid types of text, in which the 'rational' or informative features of the text dominate the coverage while highlighting the political and economic dimensions of migrant workers' identity. The text type 'emotive narrative' occupies only a very small portion of the dataset to portray the social or cultural dimensions of the migrant identity. The proportion of 'rational' to 'emotive' text types approximately parallels the ratio of political/economic dimensions to social/cultural dimensions of migrant identity accentuated. This ratifies Hodge and Kress's (1993) argument that the production of different texts reinforces the social structures, characterised by the unequal distribution of social powers. In this case, the dominant elite group (e.g. the journalists employed in the public media) has the power to employ text types that can slant the framing of different social groups to their will.

Chapter 4 described how different media participants construct various identities of, and take various stances towards, white-collar migrant workers in Chinese media discourse. To that end, this chapter took the social circulation (Spitulnik 1996) of two Chinese phrases *'he kafei'* (drinking coffee) and *'18 nian fendou'* (18 years of endeavour) concerning white collar migrant workers in Chinese media discourse as the data. These two phrases, identified as metapragmatic discourse (Silverstein 1976, 1993), use reflectivity to describe the life experience of migrant workers and have subsequently become objects of debate and public words standing for the inequality between the migrant workers and the established city dwellers in the media discourse.

This chapter revealed that authors from different social backgrounds deal with the same social issue in different ways, using different genres, linguistic devices, and social attitudes. While authors in the insiders group emotionally articulate the social inequalities between the country-born and the city-born in social life using many micro-stories and anecdotes, authors in the public intellectuals group make use of research findings and scientific data in a typical scholarly genre of exposition. Authors categorised as common outsiders attempt to re-orientate the debate towards the pursuit of a more spiritual life rather than material satisfaction. On the one hand, these differentiated stances can be seen as the products of social differences. On the other hand, the production of different texts reinforces the social structures, so the social actors can be seen as trained to adopt particular types of texts in order to maintain unequal positions of power in the society.

Chapter 5 examined how identities of migrant workers (i.e. *Nongmin Gong*) have been constructed and represented on a TV program "China's *Nongmin Gong*". Combining textual analysis of the TV talk show episodes and ethnographic fieldwork with the TV program crews, this chapter featured an in-depth exploration of the totality of this program making. This investigation found that the TV program under examination aims to construct a counter-discourse to challenge the legitimacy of the public discourse of abnormality around *Nongmin Gong* and advocates the normality or supernormality of the floating population via three distinctive stages (i.e. 'off-stage', 'back-stage', and 'front-stage') of manipulation and co-construction of the migrant workers' identity. It revealed the discursive practices and strategies employed at each stage, particularly the diverse resources and strategies the program used to transform the personal experiences of migrant workers to a form suitable for a public audience, with the purpose of fulfilling its social aim to educate the general public in China.

As a small-scale study applying a sociocultural linguistic approach to discourse analysis, Chapter 5 also drew on a wide range of theories and concepts, including sociocultural linguistic theories of identity and interaction, the dramaturgical model of social interaction, Foucault's 'abnormality', Fairclough's 'foregrounding and backgrounding', just to name a few. This fusion of theories and concepts constructed a theoretical repertoire to address the research question of the study, i.e. how the identities of migrant workers have been constructed and represented in public media in China. By employing both ethnographic and linguistic methods, this investigation has exemplified the modern interdisciplinary trend of approaching real world social issues (i.e. the public media practice in China in this book) through examination of language use, which is the sociolinguistic approach to discourse.

6.1. Media representation, interaction, and construction in Chinese contexts

In the three analytical chapters of this book, three key research questions were asked of the empirical data.

1) how do the public media in China represent the migrant workers
2) how have the media participants interacted to form public debates concerning the migrant workers
3) how have media programs discursively constructed the identities of the migrant workers.

To answer these questions, three dimensions of media practices, namely, media representation, media interaction, and media construction, all of which are closely intertwined, were explored. As a sociolinguistic investigation of media practice, the book has drawn on a diverse range of data sources and theoretical frameworks. It started with the textual analysis of representation, moved on to the analysis of interactions between media participants in forming a public debate, then proceeded with an investigation of the media discursive practices in constructing desirable identities of migrant workers. These three dimensional analyses produced a complex tapestry of the media representation and the relevant practices concerning their treatment of the migrant workers in contemporary China.

As an underprivileged social group living in the margins of society, migrant workers' mobility and social life is not likely to be a media focus in a society which traditionally values 'elites'. Consequently, we argue that the migrant workers in the media coverage under examination, have, to a great extent, been cast as the needy (i.e. the receivers of actions in its linguistic sense), passively accepting the patronage of the party, the government, and other public agents who provide care and guidance to these social inferiors. By foregrounding their political and economic values rather than their overall wellbeing, the media reflect society's attitude to this social group. Scant media coverage has placed migrant workers as the active protagonists in the media texts, rather, they are portrayed as 'the others' who are different from the normal citizens and/or are craving social care and protections.

Reference to elite people or social authorities is still the key factor by which the journalists assess the newsworthiness of an issue or event. The analysis in the book shows that the media representation of migrant workers in Chinese contexts is much inclined to portray a restricted and incomplete image of the migrant workers. This is in line with the overriding social function of the public media in China to glorify the party and its government, though, admittedly, it might also be important for the media to enhance social harmony and reconcile social tensions.

However, it would be too simplistic to assume that the privileged vs. underprivileged demarcation dominates media representation and media practice in China. Though constrained by particular political and economic powers, the public media do open up discursive spaces to a variety of social actors who take different stances towards this social disadvantaged group. However, of course, as this book indicates, such discursive spaces are not entirely open forums for all participants to vie for hegemony.

These discursive spaces have been illuminated explicitly or implicitly in different media modes in prior chapters. In Chapter 3 focusing on the print media, the Guangzhou-based *Southern Metropolis Daily* was presented as a typical newspaper that features investigative reporting and provocative commentaries. In its coverage of the migrant workers, *Southern Metropolis Daily* is the only newspaper that has attempted an overall picture of the migrant workers by emphasizing not only the political/economic but the cultural/social dimensions of their identities (see more in Chapter 3 and one sample newspaper article in Appendix I). Apparently, *Southern Metropolis Daily* regards its social function of providing balanced news as overriding its function of glorifying the party.

Collating data from both print and digital media, Chapter 4 explored the interactions between different social actors articulating their different stances towards the migrant workers and identified the key linguistic devices and genres that the social actors used to do this in this public space. Importantly, this chapter demonstrated that the public media in China, both print and digital, do in fact provide discursive spaces for social actors to present their voices. Through these fora, people from different social walks tend to compete for power and make their voices heard.

Focussing on a TV talk show program, the small-scale linguistic ethnographic study presented in Chapter 5 identified three discursive stages in the media build-up of desirable identities of migrant workers. This program was the first to invite 'real migrant workers' to the studio to present their 'real life' to the audience, thus successfully opening up the media space for this underprivileged social group to express their stories and ideas before the public, an opportunity which, though tightly controlled and manipulated, had never been offered to such people in the past.

These newly emerging media spaces, which give different social actors a chance to compete for hegemony, strongly indicate the future directions of mass media in China. In these spaces, together with the burgeoning developments of Internet and social media, the media participation of diverse social actors will not only increase, but will greatly transform the media scene in China. This trend is inevitable and irrevocable irrespective of various authoritative censorship aspects identifiable in the media.

6.2. Identities of and stances towards migrant workers in China's media

The other layer of analyses undertaken in this book was concerned with the way identity and stance are constructed through and mediated in media discourse. Identity, as understood in this book, is not something that migrant workers 'have' inherently, but something that emerges through interactional practices, especially through specific language use by different people in different media contexts for different social purposes. Identity, in this sense, is constantly produced and reproduced, delineated and designed, and often co-constructed by self and others. As argued in previous chapters, the media representation of identity is always manipulated and operationalized by the media in a way that is constrained by the institutional ideology. These manipulation and operationalization processes as well as the media representation of identities and stances have been the research foci in this book.

Identity and stance, as sociolinguistic constructs enjoying wide global attention in discourse and media studies, are much under-explored in the Chinese language and social contexts fields. This book has gone beyond the existing scholarship of identity research in Chinese media studies and has investigated media practices in the representation of migrant workers from a sociolinguistic perspective.

While finding there is a wide range of diversity in the representation of the migrant workers' identities across the public media in China, in this research some factors were found to have a greater impact on that diversity than others. For example, as shown in Chapter 3, there were clear differences between newspaper types i.e. tabloid versus party controlled broadsheets, in the stance taken towards the identity of the migrant workers. This was partly an expected finding due to the dissimilar social statuses and market orientations of these newspapers. However, an unexpected finding was that there was an even greater impact on the representation of migrants linked to geographic/regional factors. Newspapers from different regions represented the migrant workers in different ways, the differences being far greater than the differences seen between newspaper types.

Among the 278 newspaper articles analysed in Chapter 3, the majority (180 out of 278) were published by Shanghai-based newspapers with most of the migrant workers being framed as 'victims', 'trouble makers', or 'care seekers'. With a strong sense of 'otherness' attached to the workers, the local officials and the government agencies are highlighted as playing the roles of protagonists in these media articles, providing help, protection, and care to the 'foreign' migrants. It appears that Shanghai, though a long standing megacity in China's open and reform era, is still much in need of a more open-minded and tolerant attitude towards this outside human resource. Despite some concerns among the local government and the general public in Shanghai, the massive influx of migrant workers is still framed and treated as 'other' in the media discourse in that city.

This media attitude towards migrant workers as outsiders or countrymen is much in line with the longstanding ethos of Shanghainese locals, who have a well-known reputation for contempt of and discrimination against outsiders. To many older generation Shanghainese, Shanghai only consists of Shanghainese and countrymen (Chinese: 乡下人, *xiang xia ren*), the latter being the label used to refer to all people from outside Shanghai. This shallow perception of exclusiveness has undergone some changes since 1990s, when this city started to transform and expand rapidly and its people became more receptive to people from outside Shanghai, but, according to our research, the changes have not gone far enough.

The two Guangzhou-based newspapers, surprisingly, do not offer a large amount of coverage of the migrant workers, although Guangdong is the province in China holding the most migrant workers. However, as shown in Chapter 3, the outstanding feature of *Southern Metropolis Daily* is the provision of a well-balanced representation of migrant workers, portraying them mostly as 'normal' people, not much different from local workers. Unusually, their social/cultural identities are covered in these media articles as well as their political/economical identities. This projected normality (as detailed in Chapter 5) of the migrant workers is the desirable identity that a responsible society and media should pursue.

The tolerance and acceptance demonstrated towards migrant workers in the Guangzhou-based newspapers suggests that Guangdong, as a newly emerging super province in China heavily relying on the migration human resources, has developed a more open and tolerant attitude towards this 'outside' labour force. Perhaps it can be contended that Guangdong is increasingly taking migrant workers as part of its normal population rather than as some 'others' who need extra care or protection. The low overall coverage of migrant workers might also imply a recognition of migrant workers' integration into the local community, even if the relevant journalists and the media organisations are not fully aware of this. Indeed, this might reinforce Fairclough's (1993) argument that the relationships between texts and contexts are often opaque even to the participants in these communicative events. As he argues, the aims of (critical) discourse analysis are usually to systematically explore and make transparent the relationships between 1) discursive practices, events and texts, and 2) wider social and cultural structures, relations and processes.

As the political and cultural centre of China, Beijing takes a rather neutral attitude in the construction of the identities of migrant workers. Although Beijing is also a megacity holding a large population of outside migrant workers, the media in Beijing portray this social group neither with an open-minded and tolerant attitude like Guangzhou-based newspapers, nor with a narrow mindset that treats the migrant workers as social others. Their coverage of migrant workers is characterised by a strong sense of 'political correctness' focusing on themes like employment, medical and social insurance, social benefits, living conditions of migrant workers, etc.. In general, that is more a functional approach to the coverage of the migrants that still glorifies the party and the government. Similar to most of the other newspapers examined, the social and cultural dimensions of migrant workers' identity are overlooked in the media coverage of Beijing-based newspapers. However, it is surprising to note that these Beijing-based newspapers, especially the central party's organ *People's Daily*, do not follow the government advocacy of using *Xin Shimin* to refer to the migrant workers. This might suggest that the media's pursuit of market profit, now they are no longer fully subsidised by the government, has pushed them to follow suit of the general public who still prefer the use of *Nongmin Gong*, instead of fulfilling the political mission of promoting the authoritative ideology. This simple choice of language use between *Xin Shimin* and *Nongmin Gong* could involve a multiplicity of social purposes that a media institution might have to take into account.

To sum up, the media representation of the sociolinguistic constructs identity and stance is largely the product of interactions between the journalists, the authoritative ideology, the media institution, the audience, as well as the place and time of the media production. In other words, many social factors together with other tangible and intangible institutional and personal elements lead to the media representation, interaction, and construction of migrant workers' identity in the contemporary Chinese contexts.

6.3. Future directions in researching media discourse in Chinese contexts

This concluding section considers the future directions of researching media discourse in Chinese contexts. Taking into account the latest developments in technology and sociocultural milieu in China, as well as the current trends in discourse analysis and sociolinguistics, I believe there are five aspects that might be interesting to pursue in future Chinese media discourse studies.

First, the emerging social and digital media will surely be the next hot spots of media discourse research. Research would include examining the media language and discourses occurring in *Weixin* (i.e. WeChat), *Weibo* (i.e. microblogs), and other social and digital media, with a view to examining the ideology, identity, relations, and other social issues mediated in these media outlets. As rapidly increasing modes of media platforms, digital and social media have become pivotal to the life of the general public, as channels of news circulation, personal communication, entertainment, and more. The predominant social media in China include *Weibo* (microblogging, equivalent of Facebook and Twitter), especially Sina *Weibo*, Tencent Qzone (Chinese: QQ空间; equivalent of Facebook and Twitter), Tencent QQ (Instant MesSage tools), *Weixin* (i.e. WeChat, a mobile communication and private social networking app), *Renren* (Chinese: 人人网； equivalent of Facebook) and Youku and Tudou (Chinese: 优酷、土豆; equivalent of YouTube). Among them, WeChat, as one of the largest standalone messaging apps, boasting over 938 million active users across the world in 2017 (Technode 2017). As the most influential social media platform in China, this mobile app offers everything from instant calls, free video calls and group chats to news updates and sharing of large multimedia files. Its payment facility can also be used to shop online, pay physical stores, arrange deliveries, settle bills and more. It has become a hub for all internet activity of people from morning until night, from business to personal matters, and from news circulation to news production. With more in-depth information and diverse viewpoints, the language and discourse that occur on this digital platform and others (see Scotton and Hachten 2010; Shirk 2011 for an overview) will definitely become important areas of future research on Chinese media discourse.

Second, taking into account the changing dynamics between media participants, the interactions between various agents and stakeholders in media production and circulation will be an important aspect of future research (e.g. Grossberg et al. 2006; O'Keeffe 2006; Talbot 2007). With the rise of self-media and semi-independent media in China (see Huang 2000 for an overview), the conventional model of news making and circulation by institutional journalists has been significantly challenged and transformed (e.g. Zhang 2014). In the current socio-political climate in China, there is no clear distinction between government controlled and independent media. Even a publicly claimed commercial media outlet might be influenced by or have a close connection with the government. For instance, via WeChat now, common users and small groups with no media institutional fund can create news feeds on a wide range of topics, often with sensitive and in-depth information that is not commonly seen in the conventional media such as newspapers and TV programs. Even so, there are clear guidelines and strong censorship in place to control the contents of WeChat. Furthermore, in this process, the long-standing status of journalists as the sole news providers in the society has been greatly challenged, and the public media that previously solely served as the party's propaganda organ have been significantly changed. These rapidly changing relations between media makers, consumers, and other stakeholders will surely be a hot spot in future media discourse research in China.

Third, numerous social themes such as ideology, identity, stance, positioning, and alignment are deeply embedded in language use. Thus, research on media discourse cannot avoid exploring how these topics are constructed and mediated in media discourse (e.g. Bell 1991; Bell and Garrett 1998; Fairclough 1995, 2010, 2015; Fairclough et al. 2007; Johnson et al. 2007, 2010). This aligns with the current developments in discourse analysis and media studies that acknowledge language analysis and social studies are complementary to each other. On the one hand, linguistic analysis can help illuminate social and cultural research with a detailed understanding of the nature of media products. On the other hand, socioculturally orientated studies on discourse, including direct examinations of sociocultural contexts in which the language use occurs by drawing on relevant social theories, will expand and deepen conventional linguistic-oriented discourse analysis (see discussion of sociocultural linguistics and linguistic ethnography in Chapter 2). Research that draws on both linguistic and social perspectives develops an account of many real world issues and provides a window to social change and development, particularly essential in the context of massive social transformations happening in China today.

Fourth, there is an increasing trend in media discourse analysis that takes media texts as interactionally co-constructed rather than as monologue (e.g. Wang 2008; White 2004, 2006). This trend involves examining indexicality, intertextuality, intersubjectivity, evaluation, and dialogicality of media discourse and offers a perspective of both reading and writing texts as a way of looking at a text's interactions with other texts, writers, readers, and conventions. Scholars in this field look at media texts, spoken and written, as co-constructed interactionally with these elements and assume that they have the meanings which text-users assign to them in and through their interactions with other texts and media participants. These complex phenomena of discursive practices in producing and interpreting media discourse will draw growing attention from media discourse researchers.

Fifth, as a rapidly changing research area, media discourse is increasingly appropriating multimodal modes of communication to replace the traditional language-dominant mode in media coverage. These include growing use of audio, visual, and interactive modes of communication. To better understand this phenomenon, multimodal analysis of media discourse will be a new direction of future research (e.g. Jewitt 2009; Jewitt et al. 2016; Kress 2010; Kress et al. 2001). Multimodal discourse analysis has two main strands of research: one is the study of multimodality in texts such as internet webpages, newspapers, and magazines etc.; the other is the study of multimodality in spoken interactions such as interviews, and other face-to-face talk. Each area of research focus has drawn on different traditions in linguistic and social science research. While the work on the analysis of multimodality in texts has its roots in systemic functional linguistics, work on the analysis of spoken interactions has been more influenced by linguistic ethnography and ethnography of communication. These two lines of research sometimes interact, however, as media texts on web pages become more interactive (e.g. Kress 2010; Jewitt et al. 2016).

In summary, these directions of future media discourse research will, of course, be subject to the theoretical traditions and perspectives that various researchers take and the research questions that they decide to ask. What is sure, however, is that there are many areas of Chinese media discourse that deserve further exploration, and many more approaches that future researchers can appropriate.

References

Akhavan-Majid, Roya 2004. Mass media reform in China: Toward a new analytical framework. *Gazette*. 66/6, 553–565.

Bai, Fangqing 2008. Responsibility forges the brand, in *The Oral Record of China's Nongmin Gong*. Guiyang: Guizhou Education Press, 2–8.

Baidu 2017a.新市民 (*Xin Shimin*). Retrieved from <https://baike.baidu.com/item/%E6%96%B0%E5%B8%82%E6%B0%91>

Baidu 2017b. 南方都市报 (Southern Metropolis Daily). Retrieved from <https://baike.baidu.com/item/%E5%8D%97%E6%96%B9%E9%83%BD%E5%B8%82%E6 %8A%A5>

Bakhtin, Michael M. 1981. *The dialogic imagination: four essays.* Austin: University of Texas Press.

Bakhtin, Michael M. 1986. The problem of speech genres. In Emerson, C / Holquist, M (eds.). *Speech genres and other late essays.* Austin: University of Texas Press.

Barthes, Roland 1977. *Image, Music, Text (Essays selected and translated by Stephen Heath)*. New York: Hill and Wang.

Bauman, Richard 2001. Genre. In A. Duranti (ed.), *Key terms in language and culture*. Malden, MA: Blackwell, 79–82.

Bell, Allan 1991. *The language of news media*. Oxford: Blackwell.

Bell, Allan / Garrett, Peter 1998. *Approaches to media discourse.* Malden, Mass / Oxford: Blackwell.

Benwell, Bethan / Stokoe, Elizabeth 2006. *Discourse and identity.* Edinburgh: Edinburgh University Press.

Bhatia, Vijay Kumar 2004. *Worlds of written discourse: A genre-based view.* London: Continuum.

Blommaert, Jan 2005. *Discourse: A critical introduction.* Cambridge: Cambridge University Press.

Blum-Kulka, Shoshana 1997. *Dinner talk: Cultural patterns of sociability and socialization in family discourse*. Mahwah, NJ: Lawrence Erlbaum Associates.

Bois, John W. Du 2007. The stance triangle. In Robert Englebretson (ed.), *Stancetaking in discourse: Subjectivity, evaluation, interaction*. Amsterdam/Philadelphia: John Benjamins, 139–182.

Bourdieu, Pierre 1984. *Distinction: A social critique of the judgement of taste.* London: Routledge and Kegan Paul.

Bourdieu, Pierre 1992. *Language and symbolic power.* Polity Press.

Bourdieu, Pierre 2002 (1977). *Outline of a theory of practice.* Cambridge: Cambridge University Press.

Bucholtz, Mary 1999. "Why be normal?": Language and identity practices in a community of nerd girls. *Language in Society*. 28 /2, 203–223.

Bucholtz, Mary 2002. Youth and cultural practice. *Annual Review of Anthropology.* 31/1, 525–552.

Bucholtz, Mary / Hall, Kira 2004. Theorizing identity in language and sexuality research. *Language in Society*. 33/4, 469–515.

Bucholtz, Mary / Hall, Kira 2005. Identity and interaction: a sociocultural linguistic approach. *Discourse Studies.* 7/4-5, 585–614.

Bucholtz, Mary / Hall, Kira 2008. All of the above: New coalitions in sociocultural linguistics. *Journal of Sociolinguistics.* 12/ 4, 401–431.

Cai, Huajian / Sedikides, Constantine / Gaertner, Lowell / Wang, Chenjun / Carvallo, Mauricio / Xu, YiYuan / O'mara, Erin M. / Jackson, Lydia Eckstein 2011. Tactical self-enhancement in China: Is modesty at the service of self-enhancement in East Asian culture? *Social Psychological and Personality Science.* 2/1, 59–64.

Cao, Qi 2013. 新时期现代汉语变异研究 *(Research on variations of contemporary Chinese language in the new era)* (PhD thesis). Changchun: Jilin University.

Chen, Huailin / Chan, Joseph M. 1998. Bird-caged press freedom in China. In Joseph Y.S. Cheng (ed.) *China in the post-Deng era*. Hong Kong: Chinese University of Hong Kong, 645–668.

Chen, Songcen 1985. 社会语言学导论 *(Introduction to sociolinguistics),* Beijing: Peking University Press.

Chen, Songcen 1999. 语言变异研究 *(Research on Language Variation)*. Guangzhou: Guangdong Education Press.

Chu, Kejun 2010. *Framing Chinese migrant workers: A comparison of media coverage in Mainland China and Hong Kong*. Dissertation/ Thesis, ProQuest Dissertations Publishing. Iowa State University.

Clandinin, D. Jean 2007. *Handbook of narrative inquiry: mapping a methodology*. Thousand Oaks, Calif. /London: SAGE.

Connelly, F. Michael / Clandinin, D. Jean 2006. Narrative inquiry. In Green J. L. / Camilli G. / Elmore P. (eds), *Handbook of complementary methods in education research*. 3rd ed. Mahwah, NJ: Lawrence Erlbaum, 477–87.

Cortazzi, Martin 1993. *Narrative analysis*. Washington, D.C. /London: Falmer Press.

Coupland, Nikolas 2007. *Style: Language variation and identity*. Cambridge: Cambridge University Press.

Coupland, Nikolas / Jaworski, Adam (eds.) 2009. *The New Sociolinguistics Reader*, Basingstoke: Palgrave Macmillan.

Coupland, Nikolas 2016. Introduction: Sociolinguistic theory and the practice of sociolinguistics. In N. Coupland (ed.), *Sociolinguistics: Theoretical debates*. Cambridge: Cambridge University Press, 1–34. doi:10.1017/CBO9781107449787.002

Daiute, Colette / Lightfoot, Cynthia 2004. *Narrative analysis: Studying the development of individuals in society*. Thousand Oaks, Calif/ London: Sage.

De Fina, Anna / Georgakopoulou, Alexandra 2008. Analysing narratives as practices. *Qualitative Research,* 8/3, 379–387.

De Fina, Anna / Georgakopoulou, Alexandra 2012. *Analyzing narrative: discourse and sociolinguistic perspectives*. Cambridge: Cambridge University Press.

Dong, Jie 2012. When modern public space encounters postmodern migration: Abnormality and the making of migrant identities. *Sociolinguistic Studies*. 6/2, 239–257.

Endo, Tomoko 2013. Epistemic stance in Mandarin conversation: The positions and functions of *wo juede* (I feel/think). In Yuling Pan / Dániel Z. Kádár (eds.), *Chinese discourse and interaction – Theory and practice*. London: Equinox Publishing, 12–34.

Englebreton, Robert (ed.) 2007. *Stancetaking in discourse: Subjectivity, evaluation, interaction*. Amsterdam/Philadelphia: John Benjamins.

Fairclough, Norman 1993. *Discourse and social change.* Oxford: Polity Press.

Fairclough, Norman 1995. *Media discourse.* London: Edward Arnold.

Fairclough, Norman 2000. Discourse, social theory, and social research. *Journal of Sociolinguistics*, 4/2, 163–195.

Fairclough, Norman 2010. *Critical discourse analysis: The critical study of language.* 2nd edn. Harlow: Longman.

Fairclough, Norman 2012. Critical discourse analysis. In J.P. Gee / M. Handford (eds.) *The Routledge handbook of discourse analysis.* London: Routledge, 9–20.

Fairclough, Norman 2015. *Language and power.* Third edn. New York/ London: Routledge.

Fairclough, Norman / Cortese, Guiseppina / Ardizzone, Patrizia 2007. *Discourse and contemporary social change.* Bern/ Oxford: Peter Lang.

Fairclough, Norman / Wodak, Ruth 1997. Critical discourse analysis. In van Dijk, T. A. (ed.). *Discourse as social interaction*. London: Sage, 258–284.

Fan, C. Cindy 2008. *China on the move: Migration, the state, and the household.* New York/London: Routledge.

Fludernik, Monika 2009. *An introduction to narratology.* New York / London: Routledge.

Foucault, Michel 1977. *Language, counter-memory, practice: Selected essays and interviews.* Ithaca, N.Y: Cornell University Press.

Foucault, Michel 2003. *Abnormal: Lectures at the Collège de France 1974–1975.* London: Verso.

Fowler, Roger. 1991. *Language in the News: Discourse and ideology in the press.* London: Routledge.

Fulton, Helen / Huisman, Rosemary / Murphet, Julian / Dunn, Anne 2005. *Narrative and media.* Cambridge: Cambridge University Press.

Gaetano, Arianne M. / Jacka, Tamara 2004. *On the move: Women and rural-to-urban migration in contemporary China.* New York: Columbia University Press.

Garrett, Peter / Bell, Allan 1998. Media and discourse: A critical overview. In Bell, A and Garrett, P (eds.). *Approaches to media discourse*. Malden, Mass/Oxford: Blackwell.

Goffman, Erving 1956. *The presentation of self in everyday life*. Edinburgh: University of Edinburgh, Social Sciences Research Centre.

Goffman, Erving 1974. *Frame analysis: an essay on the organisation of experience*. New York: Harper and Row.

Grossberg, Lawrence / Ellen A. Wartella / D. Charles Whitney / Wise, J. Macgregor 2006. *Media making: Mass media in a popular culture*. 2nd edn. Thousand Oaks: Sage Publications.

Gumperz, John 1982. *Discourse strategies*. Cambridge: Cambridge University Press.

Gumperz, John 2001. Interactional sociolinguistics: A personal perspective, in Deborah Schiffrin / Deborah Tannen / Heidi Hamilton (eds.), *The handbook of discourse analysis*. Malden, MA: Blackwell, 215–228.

Gumperz, John / Dell Hymes (Eds.) 1972. *Directions in sociolinguistics: The ethnography of communication*. New York: Holt, Rhinehart and Winston.

Hall, Stuart 2013. The Work of Representation. In Stuart Hall / Jessica Evans / Sean Nixon (Eds.), *Representation* (2nd ed.). London: Sage, 1–15.

Hanks, William F. 1986. Authenticity and ambivalence in the text: A colonial Maya case. *American Ethnologist*. 13/4, 721–744.

Hodge, Bob / Kress, Gunther R. 1993. *Language as ideology*. 2nd edn. New York/London: Routledge.

Hoey, Micheal 1983. *On the surface of discourse*. London: George Allen and Unwin.

Huang, Chengju 2000. The development of a semi-independent press in post-Mao China: An overview and a case study of Chengdu Business News. *Journalism Studies*. 1/4, 649–664.

Hymes, Dell 1974. *Foundations in sociolinguistics: An ethnographic approach*. Philadelphia: University of Pennsylvania Press.

Hymes, Dell 1996. Report from an underdeveloped country: Toward linguistic competence in the United States. *En Current Issues in Linguistic Theory (Towards a Critical Sociolinguistics, Vol. 125)*. Philadelphia: John Benjamins Publishing Company, 150–195.

Jacka, Tamara 2005. Finding a place: Negotiations of modernization and globalization among rural women in Beijing. *Critical Asian Studies.* 37/ 1, 51–74.
Jacka, Tamara 2006. *Rural women in urban China: Gender, migration, and social change.* Armonk, N.Y: M.E. Sharpe, Inc.
Jacka, Tamara / Kipnis, Andrew B. / Sargeson, Sally 2013. *Contemporary China: Society and social change.* Port Melbourne, Vic: Cambridge University Press.
Jacka, Tamara / Sargeson, Sally 2011. *Women, gender and rural development in China.* Cheltenham, UK: Edward Elgar.
Jacquemet, Marco 2011. Crosstalk 2.0: Asylum and communicative breakdown. In Auer and Roberts (eds.) In Honour of John Gumperz. Special issue of *Text and Talk.* 31/4: 475–498.
Jaffe, Alexandra M. 2009. *Stance: Sociolinguistic perspectives.* Oxford/ New York: Oxford University Press.
Jewitt, Carey (ed.) 2009. *The Routledge handbook of multimodal analysis.* New York: Routledge.
Jewitt, Carey / Bezemer, Josephus Johannes / O'halloran, Kay L. 2016. *Introducing multimodality.* Milton Park, Abingdon/New York: Routledge.
Johnson, Sally A. / Ensslin, Astrid 2007. *Language in the media: Representations, identities, ideologies.* New York / London: Continuum.
Johnson, Sally A. / Milani, Tommaso M. 2010. *Language ideologies and media discourse: Texts, practices, politics.* New York/ London: Continuum.
Kress, Gunther 2010. *Multimodality: A social semiotic approach to contemporary communication.* London: Routledge.
Kress, Gunther / Leeuwen, Theo Van 2001. *Multimodal discourse: The modes and media of contemporary communication.* London: Hodder Arnold.
Labov, William 1963. The social motivation of a sound change. *Word.* 19:273–309.
Labov, William 1966. *The social stratification of English in New York City.* Washington, DC: Center for Applied Linguistics.
Labov, William 1969. *The study of nonstandard English.* Washington, DC: National Council of Teachers of English.

Labov, William 1972. *Sociolinguistic patterns*. Philadelphia: Pennsylvania University Press.
Labov, William 1997. Some further steps in narrative analysis. *Journal of Narrative and Life History*. 7/1–4, 395–415.
Labov, William / Fanshel, David 1977. *Therapeutic discourse: Psychotherapy as conversation*. New York: Academic Press.
Labov, William / Joshua Waletzky 1967. Narrative analysis. In J. Helm (ed.), *Essays on the Verbal and Visual Arts*. Seattle: University of Washington Press, 12–44.
Li, Yanhong 2006. 一个"差异人群"的群体素描与社会身份建构:当代城市报纸对"农民工"新闻报道的叙事分析 (Portraying a "Group of Difference": A Narrative Analysis of News Coverage on "Peasant Immigration Labour" in China's Urban Newspapers). 新闻与传播研究 *(Journalism and Communication*. 13/2, 2–14.
Li, Yanhong 2007. 新闻报道常规与弱势社群的公共表达 (News routine and public expressions of the underprivileged). *Journal of Sun Yatsen University (Social Sciences Edition)*. 47/2, 116–128.
Lorenzo-Dus, Nuria 2009. *Television discourse: Analyzing language in the media*. Basingstoke (England)/ New York: Palgrave Macmillan.
Macionis, John J. / Gerber, Linda M. 2011. *Sociology* (7th ed.). Toronto: Pearson Canada.
Martin, Jim R. 1984. Language, register and genre. In Christie, F (ed.). *Language Studies: Children's Writing: Reader*. Geelong: Deakin University Press, 21–30.
Martin, Jim R. 1997. Analysing genre: functional parameters. In Frances Christie / Jim R. *Martin* (ed.). *Genre and Institutions: Social processes in the workplace and school*. London and New York: Continuum.
Martin, Jim R. / Peters, Pam 1985. On the analysis of exposition. In R. Hasan (ed.), *Discourse on discourse: Workshop reports from the Macquarie Workshop on Discourse Analysis*. Sydney: Applied Linguistics Association of Australia, 61–92.
Martin, Jim R. / White, Peter 2007. *The language of evaluation: Appraisal in English*. Basingstoke: Palgrave Macmillan.
Miller, Carolyn R. 1984. Genre as social action. *The Quarterly Journal of Speech,* 70/ 2, 151–167.

Mishler, Elliot George 1986. *Research interviewing: Context and narrative.* Cambridge, Mass: Harvard University Press.

National Bureau of Statistics of China (2016). *2015年农民工监测调查报告 (2015 Nongmin Gong Survey Report)*. Retrieved from <http://www.stats.gov.cn/tjsj/zxfb/201604/t20160428_1349713.html>

Ochs, Elinor / Capps, Lisa 1996. Narrating the self. *Annual Review of Anthropology,* 25/1, 19–43.

O'keeffe, Anne 2006. *Investigating media discourse.* New York/London: Routledge.

Paltridge, Brian 1996. Genre, text type, and the language classroom. *ELT Journal,* 50/3, 237–243.

Pan, Yuling / Kádár, Dániel Z. 2013. *Chinese discourse and interaction: Theory and practice.* Bristol, CT/ London: Equinox.

Pan, Zhongdang / Lee, Chin-Chuan / Chan, Joseph Man / So, Clement K. Y. 2001. Orchestrating the family-nation chorus: Chinese media and nationalism in the Hong Kong handover. *Mass Communication and Society.* 4/3, 331–347. doi:10.1207/S15327825MCS0403_05

Pun, Ngai 1999. Becoming *Dagongmei* (Working Girls): The politics of identity and difference in reform China. *The China Journal.* 42: 1–18.

Rampton, Ben 2006. *Language in late modernity: Interaction in an urban school.* Cambridge: Cambridge University.

Rampton, Ben / Maybin, Janet / Roberts, Celia 2015. Theory and method in linguistic ethnography. In Snell, J / Shaw, S / Copland, F (eds.). *Linguistic ethnography: Interdisciplinary explorations*. Basingstoke: Palgrave Macmillan.

Riessman, Catherine Kohler 1993. *Narrative analysis.* Newbury Park, CA: Sage Publications.

Riessman, Catherine Kohler 2008. *Narrative methods for the human sciences.* Los Angeles: Sage Publications.

Ryan, Marie-Laure (ed.) 2004. *Narrative across media: The languages of storytelling.* Lincoln, NE: University of Nebraska Press.

Ryan, Marie-Laure 2010. Media and narrative. In Herman, DJ Manfred / Ryan, Marie-Laure (ed.). *Routledge encyclopaedia of narrative theory*. London: Routledge.

Sandelowski, Margarete 1991. Telling stories: narrative approaches in qualitative research. *Image--the Journal of Nursing Scholarship,* 23/3, 161.
Schmitter, Philippe C. 1974. Still the century of corporatism? *The Review of politics,* 36/1, 85–131.
Schryer, Catherine 2011. Investigating texts in their social contexts: the promise and peril of rhetorical genre studies, in D Starke-Meyerring / A Paré / N Artemeva / M Horne / L Yusubova (eds.), *Writing in knowledge societies: Perspectives on writing*, Fort Collins: The WAC Clearinghouse and Parlor Press, 31–52.
Schultz, Julianne 1998. *Reviving the fourth estate: Democracy, accountability and the media.* Cambridge/Melbourne: Cambridge University Press.
Scotton, James Francis / Hachten, William A. 2010. *New media for a new China.* Malden, MA/Chichester: Wiley-Blackwell.
Shirk, Susan L. 2011. *Changing media, changing China.* New York: Oxford University Press.
Shi-xu 2005. *A cultural approach to discourse.* New York: Palgrave Macmillan.
Shi-xu 2007. *Discourse as cultural struggle.* Hong Kong: Hong Kong University Press.
Shi-xu 2009. Reconstructing eastern paradigms of discourse studies. *Journal of Multicultural Discourses.* 4/1, 29–48.
Shi-xu 2010.文化话语研究： 探索中国的理论， 方法与问题 (Cultural discourse studies: Exploring Chinese theory, methods and issues). Beijing: Beijing University Press.
Shi-xu 2012. Understanding contemporary Chinese political communication: A historico-intercultural analysis and assessment of its discourse of human rights. *Journal of Language and Politics,* 11/1, 93–114.
Shuy, Roger W. 2003. A brief history of American sociolinguistics 1949–1989. In C. B. Paulston and G. R. Tucker (Eds.), *Sociolinguistics: The essential readings*. Malden, MA: Blackwell, 4–16.
Silverstein, Michael 1976. Shifters, linguistic categories and cultural description. In Basso, KH and Selby, HA (eds.). *Meaning in anthropology*. 1st. Albuquerque: University of New Mexico Press.

Silverstein, Michael 1993. Metapragmatic discourse and metapragmatic function. In Lucy, J (ed.). *Reflexive language: Reported speech and metapragmatics*. Cambridge: Cambridge University Press.

Spitulnik, Debra 1996. The social circulation of media discourse and the mediation of communities. *Journal of Linguistic Anthropology.* 6/2, 161–187.

Spolsky, Bernard 2010. Ferguson and Fishman: Sociolinguistics and the sociology of language. In R. Wodak, B. Johnstone, and P. Kerswill (eds.), *The Sage handbook of sociolinguistics*). London: Sage, 11–23.

State Council of China 2014a. 国务院关于进一步推进户籍制度改革的意见 *(State Council of China decree on further reform of the household registration system)*. Retrieved from < http://www.gov.cn/zhengce/content/2014-07/30/content_8944.htm >

State Council of China 2014b. 李克强：让农民工逐步融为城市”新市民” *(Li Keqiang: Make Nongming Gong gradually become “Xin Shimin”*. Retrieved from http://www.gov.cn/xinwen/2014-07/30/content_2727251.htm

Su Jinzhi 2010. 语言接触与语言借用：汉语借词消长研究 (Language contact and language borrowing: The fluctuating development of loan words in Chinese), 中国语言学报 *(Journal of Chinese Linguistics)* 14, 71–83.

Swales, John M. 1990. *Genre analysis: English in academic and research setting.* Cambridge, UK: Cambridge University Press.

Talbot, Mary 2007. *Media discourse: Representation and interaction.* Edinburgh: Edinburgh University Press.

Technode 2017. WeChat user and business ecosystem report 2017. Retrieved from <http://technode.com/2017/04/24/WeChat-user-business-ecosystem-report-2017/ >

Thompson, Geoff / Hunston, Susan 2000. *Evaluation in text: Authorial stance and the construction of discourse.* Oxford: Oxford University Press.

Van Dijk, Teun A. 1988. *News as discourse.* Hillsdale, NJ: Lawrence Erlbaum.

Van Dijk, Teun A. 2011. *Discourse and communication: New approaches to the analysis of mass media discourse and communication.* Berlin/ Boston: De Gruyter.

Wang, Feng/ Zuo, Xuejin 1999. Inside China's cities: Institutional barriers and opportunities for urban migrants. *American Economic Review.* 89/2, 276–280. doi:10.1257/aer.89.2.276

Wang, Wei 2007. *Newspaper commentaries in China and Australia: A contrastive genre study.* Saarbrücken, Germany: VDM Verlag Dr. Müller.

Wang, Wei 2008. Intertextual aspects of Chinese newspaper commentaries on the events of 9/11. *Discourse Studies,* 10/3, 361–381.

Wang, Wei 2014. Coffee and 18 years of endeavour: stances towards white-collar migrants in China. *Journal of Multicultural Discourses.* 9/ 2, 134–148.

Wang, Wei 2015. Co-construction of migrant workers' identities on a TV talk show in China. In Wang and Tsung (ed.), *Contemporary Chinese Discourse and Social Practice in China.* Amsterdam/ Philadelphia: John Benjamins, 125–142.

Wang, Xiaoqian 2015. 汉语自然会话中的支持性反馈研究 *(A study of supportive feedback in naturally occurring Chinese conversation).* (PhD thesis) Beijing: Minzu University of China中央民族大学

Weinreich, Uriel / Labov, William / Herzog, Marvin 1968. Empirical foundations for a theory of language change. In W. P. Lehmann / Y. Malkiel (eds.), *Directions for historical linguistics: A symposium.* Austin: University of Texas Press, 95–195.

White, Peter 2004. Subjectivity, evaluation and point of view in media discourse, in Coffin C / O'Halloran K (ed.), *Grammar, text and context: A Reader.* London / New York: Arnold, 229–257.

White, Peter 2006. Evaluative semantics and ideological positioning in journalistic discourse: A new framework for analysis, in Lassen I; Strunck J; Vestergaard T (ed.), *Mediating ideology in text and image: Ten critical studies (Discourse Approaches to Politics, Society and Culture).* Amsterdam: John Benjamins, 37–67.

White, Peter 2016. *Appraisal and media discourse.* Retrieved from http://languageofevaluation.info/appraisal/

Wodak, Ruth 2001. The discourse-historical approach. In Wodak, R and Meyer, M (eds.). *Methods of critical discourse analysis.* London: SAGE, 63–95.

Wong, Keung / Fu, Daniel / Li, Chang Ying / Song, He Xue 2007. Rural migrant workers in urban China: Living a marginalised life. *International Journal of Social Welfare.* 16/ 1, 32–40.

Wu, Doreen D. / Li, ChaoYuan / Feng, Jieyun 2016. 新媒体的社会语言学研究:回顾与展望 (Sociolinguistic studies of new media: Review and Prospect). 当代语言学*(Contemporary Linguistics)*, 4:514–531.

Xu, Daming 2002. 约翰·甘柏兹的学术思想 (John Gumperz's academic thoughts). 语言教学与研究 *(Language Teaching and Research)*. 4: 1–6.

Xu, Daming 2006. 语言变异与变化 *(Language variation and change)*. Shanghai: Shanghai Education Press.

Xu Daming / Fu Yirong 2005. 南京 '问路' 调查 (The Nanjing 'asking the way' investigation), 中国社会语言学 *(Chinese Sociolinguistics)*. 2:143–150.

Xu, Daming / Tao, Hongyin / Xie, Tianwei 1997. 当代社会语言学 *(Contemporary sociolinguistics)*. Beijing: China Social Sciences Press.

Xu, Daming / Wang Ling 2010. 城市语言调查 (Urban language investigations), 浙江大学学报（人文社会科学版） *(Journal of Zhejiang University (Humanity and Social Sciences edition)*. 6:134–140.

Xu, Feng 2000. *Women migrant workers in China's economic reform.* New York: St. Martin's Press.

Yan, Hairong 2008. *New masters, new servants: Migration, development, and women workers in China.* Durham: Duke University Press.

Young, Katharine Galloway 1987. *Tale worlds and story realms: The phenomenology of narrative.* Boston: Nijhoff.

Zhang, Qing 2005. A Chinese yuppie in Beijing: Phonological variation and the construction of a new professional identity. *Language in Society.* 32: 431–66.

Zhang, Shixin Ivy 2014. *Impact of globalization on the local press in China: A case study of the Beijing Youth Daily.* Lanham, MD: Lexington Books.
Zhao, Yuezhi 1998. *Media, market, and democracy in China: Between the party line and the bottom line*. Urbana: University of Illinois Press.
Zhao, Yuezhi 2008. *Communication in China: Political economy, power, and conflict*. Lanham, Md: Rowman and Littlefield.
Zhao, Yuezhi 2011. Understanding China's media system in a world historical context. In Hallin, DC / Mancini, P (eds.). *Comparing media systems beyond the western world.* Cambridge: Cambridge University Press.
Zhu, Wanjin 1985. 社会语言学译文集 *(Sociolinguistic papers in Chinese translation)*. Beijing: Beijing Press.
Zhu, Weihua 2016. Extended concurrent speech and *guanxi* management in Mandarin. *Text and Talk,* 36/5, 637–660.

Appendix 1

北宣恩土家族小伙李少国离家10年，从清洁工做到英语培训机构老板

到年关就急着回家 一到家又牵挂工作

日期：[2014年2月2日] 稿源：[南方都市报]

李少国带着儿子回到老家。

乡土·坐标

宣恩县地处鄂西南边陲，隶属恩施土家族苗族自治州。下辖3个镇、6个乡，县城设在珠山镇。全县总面积2740平方公里。春秋为巴子国地，清雍正十三年(1735)改土归流。乾隆元年(1736)，并施南、东乡、忠峒、忠建、木册、高罗诸土司地置县，命名宣恩。目前，全县总人口35.56万人。

宣恩属云贵高原延伸部分，地处武陵山和齐跃山的交接部位，境内自然和人文旅游资源丰富，酉水和贡水这两条古老的河流流经县域，七姊妹山上有世界著名的孑遗和观奇赏植物珙桐。

宣恩人最引以豪的是他们的土家腊肉，腊肉在锅里烹煮，香飘十里，勾人食欲，是土家人平时招待客人摆在席上的主菜之一。此外，土家油茶汤、烤洋芋、合渣、米豆腐等都是当地特色小吃。

2008年12月20日，李少国在自己的QQ空间里转发了一个名为《This is my hometown》的图集，这里面的相片，全是展现湖北省恩施土家族苗族自治州宣恩县的乡土人情。李少国说，想家的时候，这是最好的"解愁良方"。过去的10年，他在东莞过了3个年，另外的7个都回到了故乡。"每到年关时就着急地想回家，但一回到家里又开始牵挂那边(东莞长安)的工作。"李少国用"鱼和熊掌不可兼得"来形容自己复杂的乡愁。

打工第一年 穷得不敢回家过年

2003年，李少国还在宣恩一中读高二，一场突如其来的大病让他在家休学了一年。痊愈之后，他没有选择继续读书，而是跟一个

亲戚南下打工，因为家中实在太穷了，务农的父母供不起他和姐姐两人同时上学。

怀揣着800块钱，他坐上了到东莞长安的大巴。一到长安，他就赶紧出去揾工，所幸一家玩具厂录用了他。只不过，这家工厂计酬按小时算，每小时仅1.4元。在这家玩具厂，这名不满20岁的小伙子一口气从普工干到了拉长，付出的代价是每天没日没夜地干活，最多的一个月竟然上了427小时的班。

“即便如此卖力，但每个月工资才三四百元，交完100多元的生活费，根本就存不到一分钱。”李少国说，眼看就快到年关，很多工友都争相回家过年，但他自己却想都不敢想，因为身上所有的钱加起来还不够来回的车费。“一想起家里的父母和亲朋，总觉得这样回去太没面子了。”李少国说，腊月十五这天，他拿起纸笔给千里之外的父母写了一封信，告诉他们自己这一年做得还不错，并寄回去1000元钱，让父母买些好吃好喝的，但由于过年很忙回不了家过年。收到信后的父母自然是惊喜万分，但他们哪里知道，儿子已经寄出身上所有的钱，连过年都只得投靠打工的亲戚。

业余学英语　10年7次变轨

10年前的那个春节注定过得不好。但如今，当年的窘迫少年已经变成了西装革履的英语培训师，是长安当地一家小有名气的英语培训机构的老板。在过去的10年，李少国在故乡过了7个年，另外3个则留在了东莞。用李少国的话说：“只要能回就一定得回去，因为这边(广东)实在没有什么年味”。

2004年开年后，李就辞去了玩具厂的工作，选择到长安国际大酒店做清洁工。“入职时，给他们(服务员)发的是皮鞋和西服，给我发的是布鞋和马褂，当时真的觉得好失落。”李少国说，唯一让他满足的是工资变成了600元每月。在随后的日子里，这个土家小伙子还做过服务员、仓管、领班，直到后面做上了这家五星级酒店的客房主管。

2007年是李少国作了一个大胆的决定，要利用业余时间去学好英语，但这却是他学生时代最为“厌烦”的一门课。李少国说：“中学时最讨厌英语，因为怎么学都学不会，所以英语成绩是所有科目里最差的”。不过，这次虽一切从A　BCD开始，但通过勤奋的努力很快上手，“白天上班，晚上上两小时的课，回家后躺在床上继续练英语。第二天5：30起床就到出租屋后面的小山坡读英语，7：40动身去上班，就这样周而复始，坚持了一年。”李少国说。

为干一番事业，李少国又选择到英语培训班做工，并慢慢从助教做到老师，最后做到单独一所学校的负责人。2011年，有一所英语培训机构难以为继，李少国没有多想，利用自己全部积蓄将之接手了过来，并取名为“和谐外语”，既做老板又亲自担任老师。如今，“和谐外语”已经成为长安培训机构中的一个品牌，专门面向成人招生，辉煌的时候拥有3个分校。

自从辍学后南下打工，这个武陵山区走出来的土家小伙子在人生的第三个10年已完成了7次变轨。在这期间，他完成了娶妻、生子等人生大事。“我就如一只风筝，线的那一头是故乡，”李少国说，在外拼搏的日子，难免有想家的时候，开始的那几年，他一想家就只有找上几个老乡，凑在一桌吃吃饭。后来，东莞长安这边也有老乡开起了家乡饭馆，这种聚会的日子就更加多了。

除了外出的第一和第二两年，加上2008年雪灾那一年，其余每年李少国都回家过年。所谓的年味，在李少国眼中，除了家乡特色的风俗、亲友聚会外，还有就是看一看家乡每年不同的变化。

想把英语培训学校开到家乡

其实，就在《This is my hometown》这个帖子的后面，还有一个名为《计划》的帖子，李少国将自己的人生规划到72岁退休。在30-40岁这个阶段，李少国的规划是“开属于自己的分校，每两年开一家”。在李的战略蓝图里，故乡是一座绕不过的城。“我们这里穷，现在大多数成人都在外地打工，导致家里只有小孩和老人。所以小孩的教育是一个很大的问题。尤其是英语，根本无法享受到沿海地区成熟的教育资源和模式。”李少国说，自己在校没读多少书，他不愿看到孩子们步他后尘，所以打算把培训班开到宣恩，招生对象重点针对中小学生。

在李少国看来，处于武陵山区的宣恩，封闭的心态加上落后的教育模式，导致英语教学相对滞后，这也是为什么他当年不愿意学习英语的根本原因。家乡要对外交流甚至接轨国际化，无论是成人还是学生，都必须学好英语，也必须要有更开放的心态，而他正可以献出一份力量。

在李少国的空间里，写有这么一句话：“You never know what you can do till you try. If you can dream it，you can do it！”这或许便是李少国在10年里实现人生跨越的秘诀。

乡问·同题

Q：你觉得故乡最大的变化是什么？

A：我觉得故乡最大的变化是大多数人的收入及生活水平都有了很大的提升。城市建设也大变样，之前的一些菜地现在都是高楼林立了。我们是少数民族地区，自然少不了一些民族建筑，比如土家的吊脚楼等，但现在在农村地区越来越少。不过，在县城里，这类建筑却越来越多，都是政府为打造民族文化特色而兴建的，比如风雨桥、鼓楼等。不过，儿时的一些旧习俗都逐渐消失了，“汉化”已成大势所趋。比如土家的摆手舞，之前一到隆重节日，村寨内的汉子们都会到摆手堂一起跳摆手舞庆祝，如今会跳的人已为数不多。

Q：对故乡的最大愿望是什么？最担心故乡未来哪方面的发展？

A：对故乡最大的愿望是希望故乡能够继续保持高速发展，引进并开发一些新的产业让故乡变得更加富强。最担心故乡未来教育方面的发展。现在大多数成人都在外地打工，导致家里只有小孩和老人。所以小孩的教育是一个很大的问题。

Q：故乡什么事物最能寄托你的“乡愁”？

A：故乡的人最能寄托我的“乡愁”。我们宣恩是一个多民族聚居的地方，拥有土家、苗族、侗族等多个民族，我本身是土家族人，我们土家族人都非常热情、好客、淳朴。我们土家的一道特色菜就是腊猪蹄子煮火锅，如果围一桌人，全部讲着宣恩话，吃着腊蹄子，即便再远也可闻到家乡的味道。

乡情·手记

为乡愁而生

为乡愁而变

席慕蓉说：乡愁是一棵没有年轮的树，永不老去！就如李少国一样，每一个游子都有自己的乡愁。

宣恩县是一个传统的民工输出大县，在该县历年的政府工作报告中，“打工经济”都曾作为专门的一章，全县17万劳动力，常年在外务工的占到8.26万，李少国也是这打工大军中的一员。他们或怀揣着梦想，或迫于生计，踏上遥远的务工路，除了向家乡寄回辛苦钱外，还带回了先进的意识和文化，尤其是对农村地区的社会发展，推动作用不言而喻。

不过，湖北民族学院民族学和社会学学院教授刘伦文曾表示，少数民族地区农村劳动力大量流迁，对农村社会发展虽然主流是积极的，但对少数民族社会的村落经济、社会管理、当地文化和生活方式以及价值观等诸多方面却也有着负面的影响。如今，不光是学者，像李少国这样的打工者都意识到了这个问题。因此近年来，不少在外的宣恩儿女都积极加入到家乡的建设浪潮。截至2011年5月，全县农民工回乡创办的中小企业达到110多家。而在宣恩县兴起的栋栋商品楼中，购买者大部分来自外出务工者。可以说，没有这一群常年辛勤的务工者，就没有家乡如今日新月异的变化。而推动着这一股洪流涌动的背后，或许正是那浓浓的乡愁。

采写/摄影：南都记者 唐波

Translation of Appendix I

Ten years' time since Shaoguo Li, a Tujia young man from the northern Xuan'en County, left his hometown saw him transiting from a cleaner to the owner of an English language training centre

So desperate to go home at the end of the year; so concerned about the work when at home

2 February, 2014, *Southern Metropolis Daily*

Shaoguo Li brought his son back home

Home land – location

Xuan'en County is located in the far southwest of Hubei Province, China. It is under the administration of the Enshi Tujia and Miao Autonomous Prefecture. Currently, Xuan'en has three subordinate towns and six villages with the county site based in Zhushan Town. It has a total population of 355,600 residing in an area of 2,740 square kilometres. It was in the territory of Bazi in the Spring and Autumn Period (771 BC-476 BC). The territories were gradually transformed into regular districts in the 13th year (1735) of Yongzheng reign, Qing Dynasty. In the first year (1736) of Qianlong reign, the lands of headmen in Shinan, Dongxiang, Zhongdong, Zhongjian, Muce and Gaoluo were merged into a single district, which thereafter was named Xuan'en.

Xuan'en is extended part of Yunnan-Guizhou Plateau, located in the interjunction of Wuling Mountains and Qiyue Mountains, known for its abundant cultural and tourism resources. The two rivers Yaoshui and Gongshui wind through the county area from ancient times. There are famous relics and ornamental plants on the Seven Sisters, the locally well-known mountain.

Xuan'en people are proud of their Tujia preserved pork chops that are cooked in the pan. It is an appetising food with fragrance wafting miles away. It is one of the main cuisines that Tujia people serve the guests. Tujia fried tea soup, roasted potato, bean residue and rice tofu are the characteristics of the Tujia tribal special food.

On 20 December 2008 Shaoguo Li reposted a photo collection named "This Is My Hometown" in his QQ Zone. All the photos demonstrated local customs and practices of Xuan'en County, Enshi Tujia and Miao Autonomous Prefecture, Hubei Province. "This is the best cure for homesickness," Shaoguo said. During the past ten years, he went home for the Spring Festival seven times and stayed at Dongguan for three times. "I was so desperate to go home at the end of every year. However, the work over there (Chang'an town in Dongguan city) concerns me when I was home." He said. Shaoguo described his complex nostalgia as "You can't have your cake, and eat it too."

First Year of Work – Too Poor, Dare Not to Go Home for The Spring Festival

In 2003, when Shaoguo Li was in Year 11 in Yuan'en No. 1 Middle School, he was suspended for a year because of a sudden illness. He did not choose to continue education when fully recovered. Instead, he went to work in the South with a relative as the family was too poor to afford the schooling of his elder sister and himself at the same time.

He got on the bus to Chang'an, Dongguan, carrying 800 Yuan. Once he arrived at Chang'an, he quickly went out to hunt a job. Fortunately a toy factory hired him. However, he only got paid 1.4 Yuan per hour. In this toy factory, this young man under the 20 years old started to work as a general worker then became a team leader, at the cost of day and night working. He once worked 427 hours a month.

"Even worked so hard, the monthly wage was still about three to four hundred Yuan. After paying for more than 100 Yuan of living expenses, I couldn't save a penny." Shaoguo Li said. The Chinese New Year was coming soon but he couldn't do anything as all the money he had was not enough to pay the return tickets home. "When thinking of the parents, relatives and friends at home, I always feel that it's so embarrassing to go home like this." Shaoguo Li said. On the fifteenth day of the twelfth lunar month, he wrote a letter to his parents who were thousand kilometres away, saying that he had done a good job and sent 1,000 Yuan to them. He asked them to buy some delicious food and he was too busy to return home for the New Year Festival. On receiving the letter, his parents were thrilled. They didn't know that their son had sent out all his money and he had to seek refuge with a relative for the Spring Festival.

Learning English in Free Time – Seven Transitions in Ten Years

The Spring Festival 10 years ago was doomed difficult. But now, the once embarrassing boy has become a trainer of English language. He is also the owner of a local English language training institute in Chang'an with some reputation. During the past ten years, Shaoguo Li spent seven Spring Festivals in his hometown and three in Dongguan. "I have to go back home to celebrate the New Year Festival as long as I can, because Guangdong has no taste of celebration." Shaoguo Li said.

At the beginning of 2004, Li resigned from a toy factory and chose to work as a cleaner at Chang'an International Hotel. "When starting the job, they (waiters) were given leather shoes and suits, but I was given plimsolls and mandarin jacket, and I felt so lost," Shaoguo Li said. The only satisfactory thing was that his wage became 600 Yuan per month. After that, the Tujia young man also worked as a waiter, warehouse keeper, foreman and the housekeeping manager of this five-star hotel.

In 2007, Shaoguo Li made a bold decision to learn English which was the most boring subject for him when he was at school. Shaoguo Li said, "I didn't like English at all in the middle school because whatever I tried I still couldn't master it. Therefore, the results of English were the worst of all subjects." However, even though he started from the very basic of English language this time, he quickly picked it up through his hard work. "I went to work during the day, attended two hours evening class after work, and continue to practice English when I got home lying in bed. I got up at 5.30am next day to read aloud in English at the hill-side behind my rented house. Then I went out to work at 7.40am. I have kept on doing this for a year," Shaoguo Li said.

To pursue his career, Shaoguo Li decided to work for the English training classes. Starting as an assistant and then becoming a teacher, finally he was able to run a whole school independently. In 2011, an English training institute was difficult to continue the business. Shaoguo Li, without much hesitation, used up all his own savings to take it over and named it "Harmonious Foreign Language". He worked as an owner and a teacher. Now, the "Harmonious Foreign Language" has become one brand of the training centres in Chang'an, specialising for adult training. It had three branches in its premium time.

Since his dropout from school to work in the South, this Tujia young man from the Wuling Mountains has completed seven transitions in his thirties. During this period, he got married and had a son. "I was like a kite with the hometown at the other end of the line," Shaoguo Li said. In the days of hard working outside the hometown, he was inevitably homesick. At the beginning of those years, he only wanted to hang out with his countrymen for dinner together. Later, a countrymen opened a restaurant of hometown cruises and they had more opportunities to get together.

Except for the first two years when he worked outside and the winter storm in 2008, Shaoguo Li celebrated the Spring Festival at home for the other years. In the eyes of Shaoguo Li, the so-called taste of festival is the local special customs and friends and relatives gatherings as well as checking the annual changes of the hometown.

To run English Training Schools in Hometown

In fact, following the post "This is My Hometown" there is another post called "Plan" where Shaoguo Li wrote that he planned to retire at the age of 72. At the stage of 30–40 years old, he plans to "open one branch in every two years". In Li's strategic plan, the hometown is a town that he cannot avoid. "It is a poor place, most adults have been working outside. Therefore, only kids and the elders were left behind. Child education is a big problem. English education, especially is far behind the coastal areas", Shaoguo Li said. He did not have much education at school but he didn't want the children to follow his suits. He planned to set up classes in Xuan'en, mainly targeting primary and secondary school kids.

In Shaoguo Li's view, the close-mindedness and the old education system in Xuan'en County locating in Wuling Mountains caused English teaching relatively lagging behind. That was the main reason that he was not willing to study English at school. For the international exchanges and internationalization at the hometown, both adults and students must learn English, but also must have more open minds, to which he can make his contribution.

There is one sentence in Shaoguo Li's QQ Zone: "You never know what you can do till you try. If you can dream it， you can do it!" Probably it is the secret that Shaoguo Li can transcend his life in ten years.

Questions

Q: What do you think is the biggest change in your hometown?

A: I think the biggest change is that most people's income has significantly increased and living standards have been greatly improved. There is also a big change of urban construction. Now the high rises are taking the place on the former vegetable fields. We are in ethnic minority areas and there are inevitably some buildings with ethnic traits, such as Tujia Stilted Houses, which are increasingly scarce in rural areas. However, this type of buildings becomes more and more in the county sites as the government wants more constructions with ethnic cultural characteristics, such as the wind-and-rain bridge, the drum tower, etc. However, some traditional customs in my childhood have gradually disappeared. Sinicization has become a trend. For instance, the folk waving dance that the villagers used to go to the Baishoutang to celebrate on every grand festival, however, very rare people know the steps now.

Q: What is your greatest expectation for your hometown? What are you worried most about the future development of the hometown?

A: The greatest expectation would be that hometown could continue to maintain rapid development, to introduce new industries for its prosperity. I am most worried about the future education in the hometown. Now most adults are working outside with only kids and the elders at home. So the children's education is a big problem.

Q: What from your hometown can cure your homesickness?

A: The people. Our Xuan'en is a multi-ethnic place, with Tujia, Miao, Dong and other ethnic groups. I myself am a Tujia person. Our Tujia people are very warm, hospitable and honest. A special Tujia dish is called Braised Knuckle hot pot. If surrounded by a table of people who all speak the Xuan'en dialect eating this special food together, I can still smell the taste of home even it is far from the hometown.

Affections – Notes

Living for Homesickness

Changing for Homesickness

As with a poem by Xi Murong that "Homesickness is a tree without annual rings. Never grow old." Every traveller fell homesick some way as Shaoguo Li.

Lots of people in Xuan'en County continue to go out to work for many years. There is always one dedicated chapter in the county's annual government report called "Migrant Workers' Economy". The population of labour force in Xuan'en is 170,000, out of which 82,600 regularly work outside. Shaoguo Li is one of them. With pursuit of dreams and living pressure, they are looking for their fortune outside hometown. In addition to transferring hard earned money back home, they also brought back advanced technical skills and culture, which undoubtedly promotes social developments of the rural area.

However, Lunwen Liu, a professor in ethnology and sociology at Hubei Institute of Ethnicity, indicated that labour force migration from rural areas plays an active role in the rural development, but it also casts negative effects on village economy, social management, local culture, living habits and personal values. Nowadays, not only scholars, but also the migrant workers such as Shaoguo Li have realised these matters. Therefore, a few migrant workers from Xuan'en working far away from home have actively contributed to the building of their hometown. As of May 2011, over 110 middle and small sized enterprises were established by the returned migrant workers, and also most of the newly built real estate apartments in Xuan'en were purchased by them. It can be assumed that without these hard working migrant workers, the hometown cannot change so rapidly every day. The driving force of this rapid change might be the deep homesickness.

Written/photographed by Tan, Bo, Southern Metropolis Daily

Appendix II

我奋斗了18年才和你坐在一起喝咖啡
麦子

《读者》（2005第八期）

我的白领朋友们，如果我是一个初中没毕业就来沪打工的民工，你会和我坐在“星巴克”一起喝咖啡吗？不会，肯定不会。比较我们的成长历程，你会发现，为了一些在你看来唾手可得的东西，我却需要付出巨大的努力。

从我出生的一刻起，我的身份就与你有了天壤之别，因为我只能报农村户口，而你是城市户口。如果我长大以后一直保持农村户口，那么我就无法在城市中找到一份正式工作，无法享受养老保险、医疗保险。你可能会问我：“为什么非要到城市来？农村不很好吗？ 空气新鲜，又不像城市这么拥挤。”可是农村没有好的医疗条件，去年SARS好像让大家一夜之间发现农村的医疗保健体系竟然如此落后，物质供应也不丰富，因为农民挣的钱少，贵一点儿的东西就买不起，所以商贩也不会进太多货。春节联欢晚会的小品中买得起等离子彩电的农民毕竟是个别现象，绝大多数农民还在为基本的生存而奋斗，于是我要进城，要通过自己的奋斗获得你生下来就拥有的大城市户口。

考上大学是我跳出农门的惟一机会。我要刻苦学习，小学升初中，初中升高中，高中考大学，我在独木桥上奋勇搏杀，眼看着周围的同学一批批落马，前面的道路越来越窄，我这个佼佼者心里不知是喜是忧。激烈的竞争让我不敢疏忽，除了学习功课，我无暇顾及业余爱好，学校也没有这些发展个人特长的课程。进入高中的第一天，校长就告诉我们这三年只有一个目标——高考。于是我披星戴月，早上5：30起床，晚上 11：00睡觉，就连中秋节的晚上，我还在路灯下背政治题。

而你的升学压力要小得多，竞争不是那么激烈，功课也不是很沉重，你可以有充足的时间去发展个人爱好，去读课外读物，去球场挥汗如雨，去野外享受蓝天白云。如果你不想那么辛苦去参加高考，只要成绩不是太差，你可以在高三时有机会获得保送名额，哪怕成绩忒差，也会被“扫”进一所本地三流大学，而那所三流大学我可能也要考到很高的分数才能进去，因为按地区分配的名额中留给上海本地的名额太多了。

我们的考卷一样我们的分数线却不一样，但是当我们都获得录取通知书的时候，所交的学费是一样的。每人每年6000元，四年下来光学费就要2.4万元，再加上住宿费每人每年1500元，还有书本教材费每年1000元、生活费每年4000元（只吃学校食堂），四年总共5万元。2003年上海某大学以“新建的松江校区环境优良”为由，将学费提高到每人每年1万元，这就意味着仅学费一项四年就要4万元，　再加上其他费用，总共6.6万元。6.6万元对于一个上海城市家庭来说也许算不上沉重的负担，可是对于一个农村的家庭，这简直是一辈子的积蓄。我的家乡在　东部沿海开放省份，是一个农业大省，相比西部内陆省份应该说经济水平还算比较好，但一年辛苦劳作也剩不了几个钱。以供养两个孩子的四口之家为例，除去各种　日常必需开支，一个家庭每年最多积蓄3000元，那么6.6万元上大学的费用意味着22年的积蓄！前提是任何一个家庭成员都不能生大病，而且另一个孩子无论学习成绩多么优秀，都必须剥夺他上大学的权利，因为家里只能提供这么多钱。我属于比较幸运的，东拼西凑加上助学贷款终于交齐了第一年的学费，看着那些握着录取通知书愁苦不堪全家几近绝望的同学，我的心中真的不是滋味。教育产业化时代的大学招收的?

我终于可以如愿以偿地在大学校园里汲取知识的养分！努力学习获得奖学金，假期打工挣点生活费，我实在不忍心多拿父母一分钱，那每一分钱都是一滴汗珠掉在地上摔成八瓣挣来的血汗钱啊！

来到上海这个大都市，我发现与我的同学相比我真是土得掉渣。我不会作画，不会演奏乐器，不认识港台明星，没看过武侠小说，不认得MP3，不知道什么是walkman，为了弄明白营销管理课上讲的“仓储式超市”的概念，我在“麦德隆”好奇地看了一天，我从来没见过如此丰富的商品。

我没摸过计算机，为此我花了半年时间泡在学校机房里学习你在中学里就学会的基础知识和操作技能。我的英语是聋子英语、哑巴英语，我的发音中国人和外国人都听不懂，这也不能怪我，我们家乡没有外教，老师自己都读不准，怎么可能教会学生如何正确发音？基础没打好，我只能再花一年时间矫正我的发音。我真的很羡慕大城市的同学多才多艺，知识面那么广，而我只会读书，我的学生时代只有学习、考试、升学， 因为只有考上大学，我才能来到你们中间，才能与你们一起学习，所有的一切都必须服从这个目标。

我可以忍受城市同学的嘲笑，可以几个星期不吃一份荤菜，可以周六周日全天泡在图书馆和自习室，可以在周末自习回来的路上羡慕地看着校园舞厅里的成双成对，可以在寂寞无聊的深夜在操场上一圈圈地奔跑。我想有一天我毕业的时候，我能在这个大都市挣一份工资的时候，我会和你这个生长在都市里的同龄人一样——做一个上海公民，而我的父母也会为我骄傲，因为他们的孩子在大上海工作！

终于毕业了，在上海工作难找，回到家乡更没有什么就业机会。(能幸运地在上海找到工作的应届本科生只有每月2000元左右的工资水平，也许你认为这点钱应该够你零花的了，可是对我来说，我还要租房，还要交水电煤电话费还要还助学贷款，还想给家里寄点钱让弟妹继续读书，剩下的钱只够我每顿吃盖浇饭，我还是不能与你坐在“星巴克”一起喝咖啡！

如今的我在上海读完了硕士，现在有一份年薪七八万的工作。我奋斗了18年，现在终于可以与你坐在一起喝咖啡。我已经融入到这个国际化大都市中了，与周围的白领朋友没有什么差别。可是我无法忘记奋斗历程中那些艰苦的岁月，无法忘记那些曾经的同学和他们永远无法实现的夙愿。于是我以第一人称的方式写下了上面的文字，这些是最典型的中小城市和农村平民子弟奋斗历程的写照。每每看到正在同命运抗争的学子，我的心里总是会有一种沉重的责任感。

写这篇文章不是为了怨天尤人，这个世界上公平是相对的，这并不可怕，但是对不公平视而不见是非常可怕的。我在上海读硕士的时候，曾经讨论过一个维达纸业的营销案例，我的一位当时曾有三年工作经验，现任一家中外合资公司人事行政经理的同学，提出一个方案：应该让维达纸业开发高档面巾纸产品推向9亿农民市场。我惊讶于她提出这个方案的勇气，当时我问她是否知道农民兄弟吃过饭后如何处理面部油腻，她疑惑地看着我，我用手背在两侧嘴角抹了两下，对如此不雅的动作她投以鄙夷神色。

在一次宏观经济学课上，我的另一同学大肆批判下岗工人和辍学务工务农的少年：“80%是由于他们自己不努力，年轻的时候不学会一门专长，所以现在下岗活该！那些学生可以一边读书一边打工嘛，据说有很多学生一个暑假就能赚几千元，学费还用愁吗？”我的这位同学太不了解贫困地区农村了。

我是70年代中期出生的人，我的同龄人正在逐渐成为社会的中流砥柱，我们的行为将影响社会和经济的发展。把这篇文章送给那些在优越环境中成长起来的年轻人和很久以前曾经吃过苦现在已经淡忘的人，关注社会下层，为了这个世界更公平些，我们应该做些力所能及的事情，让社会责任感驻留我们的头脑。

我花了18年时间才能和你坐在一起喝咖啡。

Translation of Appendix II

I'm finally able to drink coffee together with you after 18 years of endeavour

Maizi
Duzhe, Issue 8, 2005

My white-collar friends, if I was a migrant worker who came to work in Shanghai just after junior high school, will you sit down with me for "Starbucks" coffee? No, definitely not. Comparing our growth courses, you will find something at your fingertips will cost my big efforts.

From the moment of my birth, my identity and yours have a great gap, because I can only be on a rural *hukou*, and you have been on a city one. If remaining on a rural *hukou* I won't find an official working position in the city, unable to enjoy the old-age pension and medical insurance when I grow up. You might ask me: "why cities? Isn't it good in rural areas? There is fresh air, unlike the city, so crowded." But there are no good healthcare facilities in rural areas. SARS last year seems to make you aware overnight that the rural health care system is so backward without sufficient material supply. As the farmers earn less money, little things they just can't afford, so traders don't keep much in stock. The farmers in the Spring Festival TV Gala Show, who can afford plasma TV, after all, are isolated cases. The vast majority of farmers are still struggling for basic survival, and so I want to go to the city, by my own efforts, to gain a city *hukou* which you attained at birth.

The university is the only chance for me to jump out of the farm. I have to study hard, primary to junior high school, junior to senior high school, high school to university. I was struggling on the single-plank bridge, seeing the students keep falling off the bridge while the road ahead is getting narrower. As the lucky one, I am filled with contentment and anxiety. Fierce competition kept me highly alert. Except learning hard, I have no time to take care of hobbies, and schools didn't offer courses for personal development. The first day into the senior high school, the principal told us that there is only one goal in these three years – university entrance examination. So I studied around the clock, getting up at 5:30am, going to bed at 11:00 at night. Even at night of the Mid-Autumn Festival, I was still under the street lights memorising politics questions.

While your school pressure is much less, the competition not so intense, homework not very heavy, you can have enough time to develop personal hobbies, to do extracurricular reading, to play in the stadium, to enjoy the blue sky and white clouds in the wild. If you do not want to go so hard to participate in the university entrance examination, with above-average scores you might get a position of automatic transfer to university. Even with the substandard results, you can be "swept" into a local third-rate university, which I might need a very high score to be admitted, because there are too many university positions allocated by the region to Shanghai.

Our exam papers are the same but not our admission scores. However, the tuition fees are the same when we get the offer. With 6000 *Yuan* per person per year, four years will mean 24,000 *Yuan*, plus accommodation costs of 1,500 *Yuan* per person per year. There are also book costs of 1,000 *Yuan* per year, and the living cost of 4,000 *Yuan* per year (eat at the school canteen). A total of 50,000 *Yuan* for four years. In 2003 a university in Shanghai increased the tuition fee to 10,000 *Yuan* with the reason of "good environments in the new *Songjiang* campus", which means that only the four years tuition will be 40,000 *Yuan*. Plus other costs, the total will be 66,000 *Yuan*, which for a Shanghai urban family may not be a heavy burden. But for a rural family, this will be a lifetime savings. My hometown is a large agricultural province in the eastern coast. Compared with the western inland provinces, its economic level is still better. But hard labour in a year cannot save much money. For a family of four with two kids, to deduct the daily necessities, a family can save up 3,000 *Yuan* maximum a year. Then the 66,000 *Yuan* university cost means 22 years of savings! The premise is that any family member cannot get sick, and another child, no matter how good his/her academic performance, must be deprived of university rights, because the family can only provide so much money. I am among the lucky ones whose savings plus student loans can finally pay the first year tuition. Seeing those desperate students holding the admission letters with sad and unbearable families, my heart is filled with pain. Which students will the universities enroll in the commercialised era of education?

I have finally realised my wish of learning new knowledge on the university campus! Studying hard to get scholarships, earning living expenses with a job in vacations, I really cannot bear to take my parents a penny, that every penny is a drop of sweat falling onto the ground!

Upon my arrival in Shanghai, the largest city, I found that I was always stupid and unenlightened in comparison with my classmates. I'm unable to paint, unable to play a musical instrument, do not recognise Taiwan and Hong Kong pop stars, have not read Kung Fu novels, do not know the MP3, and I do not know what is a Walkman. In order to sort out the concept of "warehouse supermarket" taught in the marketing management course, I was wandering in "*Maidelong* supermarket" curiously for a whole day, in which I have never seen so much merchandise before.

As having never touched the computer before, I have to spend half a year to learn the basics and the operational skills, which you have learned in the secondary school. With my 'deaf and dumb' English, my English pronunciation is not comprehensible by either Chinese or foreigners. I cannot be blamed, as there are no foreign teachers in our hometown, and the teachers themselves cannot pronounce correctly, let alone their students. Without good foundation, I have to spend another year to correct my pronunciation. I really envy the big city students' versatility and broad knowledge, but I can only study. My student age is filled with only study, examination, and university admission. As only being admitted to the university, I can come to you and study with you. Everything must comply with this goal.

I can endure the mockery of the city students, eat without meat for a few weeks, study all day on weekend in the library or study rooms, envy the happy pairs in the school ballroom on my way back to the dormitory in the weekend, and even run in circles of the sports ground lonely at night. I would like, one day when I graduate, to earn a salary in this metropolis. I will, as you growing up in this city, be a Shanghai citizen, and my parents will be proud of me, because their children are working in big Shanghai!

Finally graduated, it is difficult to find a job in Shanghai, and there are no more job opportunities back at hometown. For those fresh graduates who are lucky to find a job in Shanghai, they can only earn 2000 *Yuan* per month. You may think this money should be enough for your pocket money. But for me, with it I have to pay rental, bills for water, electricity, gas and telephone, also pay back the student loan. Besides, I also wanted to send some money home for brothers and sisters' schooling. What is left is scarcely enough for me to cover my quick meals. Still I am unable to have coffee with you in Starbucks!

Today I have completed my master degree in Shanghai and now have had a job with an annual salary of seventy or eighty thousands. I have struggled for 18 years, and now finally can sit with you to drink coffee. I have been integrated into this international metropolis, and with no difference to the white-collar friends around. But I cannot forget the hardships of those struggling years, cannot forget those former schoolmates who can never achieve their long-cherished goals. So I wrote the above text in the first person, which is the most typical portrayal of a struggling kid from small and medium-sized cities and rural areas. Often viewing their fight with the fate, my heart is always filled with a heavy sense of responsibility.

Writing this article is not to blame the world for fairness, which is always relative. But it is terrible to turn a blind eye on it. When I was doing my master degree in Shanghai, we discussed a marketing case for the *Weida Paper*. One of my former classmates with three years of work experience (now she is a HR manager in a joint venture) proposed a marketing plan that *Weida Paper* should develop high-grade tissue paper products for the farmers market with 900 million population. I was amazed at the courage of her proposal. Then I asked her whether she knew how the peasant brothers dealt with the meal grease, and she looked at me with puzzles. I wiped my hand on both sides of my mouth and on such action she cast a contemptuous look.

In a macroeconomics class, another classmate of mine criticized laid-off workers and teenagers who had quit their schooling for jobs: "80% of them are because they did not work hard, they do not learn a skill when they are young, so they deserve being laid-off! For those students, they can work while studying. Well, it is said that many students can earn thousands during a summer vacation. Why are they worried about the tuition?" My classmate didn't understand the poor rural areas.

I was born in the mid-1970s. My peers are gradually becoming the mainstay of society, and our behaviors will affect the social and economic developments. This article is presented to those young people who grew up in a superior environment and those who have had bitter experience a long time ago but forgotten now. With a view to caring about the lower classes of society and better social justice in the world, we should do whatever we can, bearing responsibility in our minds.

I'm finally able to drink coffee together with you upon 18 years of endeavour.

Index

Linguistic Insights

Studies in Language and Communication

This series aims to promote specialist language studies in the fields of linguistic theory and applied linguistics, by publishing volumes that focus on specific aspects of language use in one or several languages and provide valuable insights into language and communication research. A cross-disciplinary approach is favoured and most European languages are accepted.

The series includes two types of books:

- **Monographs** – featuring in-depth studies on special aspects of language theory, language analysis or language teaching.
- **Collected papers** – assembling papers from workshops, conferences or symposia.

Each volume of the series is subjected to a double peer-reviewing process.

Vol. 1 Maurizio Gotti & Marina Dossena (eds)
Modality in Specialized Texts. Selected Papers of the 1st CERLIS Conference.
421 pages. 2001. ISBN 3-906767-10-8 · US-ISBN 0-8204-5340-4

Vol. 2 Giuseppina Cortese & Philip Riley (eds)
Domain-specific English. Textual Practices across Communities and Classrooms.
420 pages. 2002. ISBN 3-906768-98-8 · US-ISBN 0-8204-5884-8

Vol. 3 Maurizio Gotti, Dorothee Heller & Marina Dossena (eds)
Conflict and Negotiation in Specialized Texts. Selected Papers of the 2nd CERLIS Conference.
470 pages. 2002. ISBN 3-906769-12-7 · US-ISBN 0-8204-5887-2

Vol. 4 Maurizio Gotti, Marina Dossena, Richard Dury, Roberta Facchinetti & Maria Lima
Variation in Central Modals. A Repertoire of Forms and Types of Usage in Middle English and Early Modern English.
364 pages. 2002. ISBN 3-906769-84-4 · US-ISBN 0-8204-5898-8

Editorial address:

Prof. Maurizio Gotti — Università di Bergamo, Dipartimento di Lingue, Letterature Straniere e Comunicazione, Piazza Rosate 2, 24129 Bergamo, Italy
Fax: +39 035 2052789, E-Mail: m.gotti@unibg.it

Vol. 5 Stefania Nuccorini (ed.)
Phrases and Phraseology. Data and Descriptions.
187 pages. 2002. ISBN 3-906770-08-7 · US-ISBN 0-8204-5933-X

Vol. 6 Vijay Bhatia, Christopher N. Candlin & Maurizio Gotti (eds)
Legal Discourse in Multilingual and Multicultural Contexts.
Arbitration Texts in Europe.
385 pages. 2003. ISBN 3-906770-85-0 · US-ISBN 0-8204-6254-3

Vol. 7 Marina Dossena & Charles Jones (eds)
Insights into Late Modern English. 2nd edition.
378 pages. 2003, 2007.
ISBN 978-3-03911-257-9 · US-ISBN 978-0-8204-8927-8

Vol. 8 Maurizio Gotti
Specialized Discourse. Linguistic Features and Changing Conventions.
351 pages. 2003, 2005.
ISBN 3-03910-606-6 · US-ISBN 0-8204-7000-7

Vol. 9 Alan Partington, John Morley & Louann Haarman (eds)
Corpora and Discourse.
420 pages. 2004. ISBN 3-03910-026-2 · US-ISBN 0-8204-6262-4

Vol. 10 Martina Möllering
The Acquisition of German Modal Particles. A Corpus-Based Approach.
290 pages. 2004. ISBN 3-03910-043-2 · US-ISBN 0-8204-6273-X

Vol. 11 David Hart (ed.)
English Modality in Context. Diachronic Perspectives.
261 pages. 2003. ISBN 3-03910-046-7 · US-ISBN 0-8204-6852-5

Vol. 12 Wendy Swanson
Modes of Co-reference as an Indicator of Genre.
430 pages. 2003. ISBN 3-03910-052-1 · US-ISBN 0-8204-6855-X

Vol. 13 Gina Poncini
Discursive Strategies in Multicultural Business Meetings.
2nd edition. 338 pages. 2004, 2007.
ISBN 978-3-03911-296-8 · US-ISBN 978-0-8204-8937-7

Vol. 14 Christopher N. Candlin & Maurizio Gotti (eds)
Intercultural Aspects of Specialized Communication.
2nd edition. 369 pages. 2004, 2007.
ISBN 978-3-03911-258-6 · US-ISBN 978-0-8204-8926-1

Vol. 15 Gabriella Del Lungo Camiciotti & Elena Tognini Bonelli (eds)
Academic Discourse. New Insights into Evaluation.
234 pages. 2004. ISBN 3-03910-353-9 · US-ISBN 0-8204-7016-3

Vol. 16 Marina Dossena & Roger Lass (eds)
Methods and Data in English Historical Dialectology.
405 pages. 2004. ISBN 3-03910-362-8 · US-ISBN 0-8204-7018-X

Vol. 17 Judy Noguchi
The Science Review Article. An Opportune Genre in
the Construction of Science.
274 pages. 2006. ISBN 3-03910-426-8 · US-ISBN 0-8204-7034-1

Vol. 18 Giuseppina Cortese & Anna Duszak (eds)
Identity, Community, Discourse. English in Intercultural Settings.
495 pages. 2005. ISBN 3-03910-632-5 · US-ISBN 0-8204-7163-1

Vol. 19 Anna Trosborg & Poul Erik Flyvholm Jørgensen (eds)
Business Discourse. Texts and Contexts.
250 pages. 2005. ISBN 3-03910-606-6 · US-ISBN 0-8204-7000-7

Vol. 20 Christopher Williams
Tradition and Change in Legal English. Verbal Constructions in Prescriptive Texts.
2nd revised edition. 216 pages. 2005, 2007. ISBN 978-3-03911-444-3.

Vol. 21 Katarzyna Dziubalska-Kolaczyk & Joanna Przedlacka (eds)
English Pronunciation Models: A Changing Scene.
2nd edition. 476 pages. 2005, 2008. ISBN 978-3-03911-682-9.

Vol. 22 Christián Abello-Contesse, Rubén Chacón-Beltrán, M. Dolores López-Jiménez & M. Mar Torreblanca-López (eds)
Age in L2 Acquisition and Teaching.
214 pages. 2006. ISBN 3-03910-668-6 · US-ISBN 0-8204-7174-7

Vol. 23 Vijay K. Bhatia, Maurizio Gotti, Jan Engberg & Dorothee Heller (eds)
Vagueness in Normative Texts.
474 pages. 2005. ISBN 3-03910-653-8 · US-ISBN 0-8204-7169-0

Vol. 24 Paul Gillaerts & Maurizio Gotti (eds)
Genre Variation in Business Letters. 2nd printing.
407 pages. 2008. ISBN 978-3-03911-681-2.

Vol. 25 Ana María Hornero, María José Luzón & Silvia Murillo (eds)
Corpus Linguistics. Applications for the Study of English.
2nd printing. 526 pages. 2006, 2008. ISBN 978-3-03911-726-0

Vol. 26 J. Lachlan Mackenzie & María de los Ángeles Gómez-González (eds)
Studies in Functional Discourse Grammar.
259 pages. 2005. ISBN 3-03910-696-1 · US-ISBN 0-8204-7558-0

Vol. 27 Debbie G. E. Ho
Classroom Talk. Exploring the Sociocultural Structure of Formal ESL Learning.
2nd edition. 254 pages. 2006, 2007. ISBN 978-3-03911-434-4

Vol. 28 Javier Pérez-Guerra, Dolores González-Álvarez, Jorge L. Bueno-Alonso & Esperanza Rama-Martínez (eds)
'Of Varying Language and Opposing Creed'. New Insights into Late Modern English.
455 pages. 2007. ISBN 978-3-03910-788-9

Vol. 29 Francesca Bargiela-Chiappini & Maurizio Gotti (eds)
Asian Business Discourse(s).
350 pages. 2005. ISBN 3-03910-804-2 · US-ISBN 0-8204-7574-2

Vol. 30 Nicholas Brownlees (ed.)
News Discourse in Early Modern Britain. Selected Papers of CHINED 2004.
300 pages. 2006. ISBN 3-03910-805-0 · US-ISBN 0-8204-8025-8

Vol. 31 Roberta Facchinetti & Matti Rissanen (eds)
Corpus-based Studies of Diachronic English.
300 pages. 2006. ISBN 3-03910-851-4 · US-ISBN 0-8204-8040-1

Vol. 32 Marina Dossena & Susan M. Fitzmaurice (eds)
Business and Official Correspondence. Historical Investigations.
209 pages. 2006. ISBN 3-03910-880-8 · US-ISBN 0-8204-8352-4

Vol. 33 Giuliana Garzone & Srikant Sarangi (eds)
Discourse, Ideology and Specialized Communication.
494 pages. 2007. ISBN 978-3-03910-888-6

Vol. 34 Giuliana Garzone & Cornelia Ilie (eds)
The Use of English in Institutional and Business Settings.
An Intercultural Perspective.
372 pages. 2007. ISBN 978-3-03910-889-3

Vol. 35 Vijay K. Bhatia & Maurizio Gotti (eds)
Explorations in Specialized Genres.
316 pages. 2006. ISBN 3-03910-995-2 · US-ISBN 0-8204-8372-9

Vol. 36 Heribert Picht (ed.)
Modern Approaches to Terminological Theories and Applications.
432 pages. 2006. ISBN 3-03911-156-6 · US-ISBN 0-8204-8380-X

Vol. 37 Anne Wagner & Sophie Cacciaguidi-Fahy (eds)
Legal Language and the Search for Clarity / Le langage juridique et la quête de clarté.
Practice and Tools / Pratiques et instruments.
487 pages. 2006. ISBN 3-03911-169-8 · US-ISBN 0-8204-8388-5

Vol. 38 Juan Carlos Palmer-Silveira, Miguel F. Ruiz-Garrido &
Inmaculada Fortanet-Gómez (eds)
Intercultural and International Business Communication.
Theory, Research and Teaching.
2nd edition. 343 pages. 2006, 2008. ISBN 978-3-03911-680-5

Vol. 39 Christiane Dalton-Puffer, Dieter Kastovsky, Nikolaus Ritt &
Herbert Schendl (eds)
Syntax, Style and Grammatical Norms. English from 1500–2000.
250 pages. 2006. ISBN 3-03911-181-7 · US-ISBN 0-8204-8394-X

Vol. 40 Marina Dossena & Irma Taavitsainen (eds)
Diachronic Perspectives on Domain-Specific English.
280 pages. 2006. ISBN 3-03910-176-0 · US-ISBN 0-8204-8391-5

Vol. 41 John Flowerdew & Maurizio Gotti (eds)
Studies in Specialized Discourse.
293 pages. 2006. ISBN 3-03911-178-7

Vol. 42 Ken Hyland & Marina Bondi (eds)
Academic Discourse Across Disciplines.
320 pages. 2006. ISBN 3-03911-183-3 · US-ISBN 0-8204-8396-6

Vol. 43 Paul Gillaerts & Philip Shaw (eds)
The Map and the Landscape. Norms and Practices in Genre.
256 pages. 2006. ISBN 3-03911-182-5 · US-ISBN 0-8204-8395-4

Vol. 44 Maurizio Gotti & Davide Giannoni (eds)
New Trends in Specialized Discourse Analysis.
301 pages. 2006. ISBN 3-03911-184-1 · US-ISBN 0-8204-8381-8

Vol. 45 Maurizio Gotti & Françoise Salager-Meyer (eds)
Advances in Medical Discourse Analysis. Oral and Written Contexts.
492 pages. 2006. ISBN 3-03911-185-X · US-ISBN 0-8204-8382-6

Vol. 46 Maurizio Gotti & Susan Šarcević (eds)
Insights into Specialized Translation.
396 pages. 2006. ISBN 3-03911-186-8 · US-ISBN 0-8204-8383-4

Vol. 47 Khurshid Ahmad & Margaret Rogers (eds)
Evidence-based LSP. Translation, Text and Terminology.
584 pages. 2007. ISBN 978-3-03911-187-9

Vol. 48 Hao Sun & Dániel Z. Kádár (eds)
It's the Dragon's Turn. Chinese Institutional Discourses.
262 pages. 2008. ISBN 978-3-03911-175-6

Vol. 49 Cristina Suárez-Gómez
Relativization in Early English (950-1250). the Position of Relative Clauses.
149 pages. 2006. ISBN 3-03911-203-1 · US-ISBN 0-8204-8904-2

Vol. 50 Maria Vittoria Calvi & Luisa Chierichetti (eds)
Nuevas tendencias en el discurso de especialidad.
319 pages. 2006. ISBN 978-3-03911-261-6

Vol. 51 Mari Carmen Campoy & María José Luzón (eds)
Spoken Corpora in Applied Linguistics.
274 pages. 2008. ISBN 978-3-03911-275-3

Vol. 52 Konrad Ehlich & Dorothee Heller (Hrsg.)
Die Wissenschaft und ihre Sprachen.
323 pages. 2006. ISBN 978-3-03911-272-2

Vol. 53 Jingyu Zhang
The Semantic Salience Hierarchy Model. The L2 Acquisition of Psych Predicates
273 pages. 2007. ISBN 978-3-03911-300-2

Vol. 54 Norman Fairclough, Giuseppina Cortese & Patrizia Ardizzone (eds)
Discourse and Contemporary Social Change.
555 pages. 2007. ISBN 978-3-03911-276-0

Vol. 55 Jan Engberg, Marianne Grove Ditlevsen, Peter Kastberg & Martin Stegu (eds)
New Directions in LSP Teaching.
331 pages. 2007. ISBN 978-3-03911-433-7

Vol. 56 Dorothee Heller & Konrad Ehlich (Hrsg.)
Studien zur Rechtskommunikation.
322 pages. 2007. ISBN 978-3-03911-436-8

Vol. 57 Teruhiro Ishiguro & Kang-kwong Luke (eds)
Grammar in Cross-Linguistic Perspective.
The Syntax, Semantics, and Pragmatics of Japanese and Chinese.
304 pages. 2012. ISBN 978-3-03911-445-0

Vol. 58 Carmen Frehner
Email – SMS – MMS
294 pages. 2008. ISBN 978-3-03911-451-1

Vol. 59 Isabel Balteiro
The Directionality of Conversion in English. A Dia-Synchronic Study.
276 pages. 2007. ISBN 978-3-03911-241-8

Vol. 60 Maria Milagros Del Saz Rubio
English Discourse Markers of Reformulation.
237 pages. 2007. ISBN 978-3-03911-196-1

Vol. 61 Sally Burgess & Pedro Martín-Martín (eds)
English as an Additional Language in Research Publication and Communication.
259 pages. 2008. ISBN 978-3-03911-462-7

Vol. 62 Sandrine Onillon
Pratiques et représentations de l'écrit.
458 pages. 2008. ISBN 978-3-03911-464-1

Vol. 63 Hugo Bowles & Paul Seedhouse (eds)
Conversation Analysis and Language for Specific Purposes.
2nd edition. 337 pages. 2007, 2009. ISBN 978-3-0343-0045-2

Vol. 64 Vijay K. Bhatia, Christopher N. Candlin & Paola Evangelisti Allori (eds)
Language, Culture and the Law.
The Formulation of Legal Concepts across Systems and Cultures.
342 pages. 2008. ISBN 978-3-03911-470-2

Vol. 65 Jonathan Culpeper & Dániel Z. Kádár (eds)
Historical (Im)politeness.
300 pages. 2010. ISBN 978-3-03911-496-2

Vol. 66 Linda Lombardo (ed.)
Using Corpora to Learn about Language and Discourse.
237 pages. 2009. ISBN 978-3-03911-522-8

Vol. 67 Natsumi Wakamoto
Extroversion/Introversion in Foreign Language Learning.
Interactions with Learner Strategy Use.
159 pages. 2009. ISBN 978-3-03911-596-9

Vol. 68 Eva Alcón-Soler (ed.)
Learning How to Request in an Instructed Language Learning Context.
260 pages. 2008. ISBN 978-3-03911-601-0

Vol. 69 Domenico Pezzini
The Translation of Religious Texts in the Middle Ages.
428 pages. 2008. ISBN 978-3-03911-600-3

Vol. 70 Tomoko Tode
Effects of Frequency in Classroom Second Language Learning.
Quasi-experiment and stimulated-recall analysis.
195 pages. 2008. ISBN 978-3-03911-602-7

Vol. 71 Egor Tsedryk
Fusion symétrique et alternances ditransitives.
211 pages. 2009. ISBN 978-3-03911-609-6

Vol. 72 Cynthia J. Kellett Bidoli & Elana Ochse (eds)
English in International Deaf Communication.
444 pages. 2008. ISBN 978-3-03911-610-2

Vol. 73 Joan C. Beal, Carmela Nocera & Massimo Sturiale (eds)
Perspectives on Prescriptivism.
269 pages. 2008. ISBN 978-3-03911-632-4

Vol. 74 Carol Taylor Torsello, Katherine Ackerley & Erik Castello (eds)
Corpora for University Language Teachers.
308 pages. 2008. ISBN 978-3-03911-639-3

Vol. 75 María Luisa Pérez Cañado (ed.)
English Language Teaching in the European Credit Transfer System.
Facing the Challenge.
251 pages. 2009. ISBN 978-3-03911-654-6

Vol. 76 Marina Dossena & Ingrid Tieken-Boon van Ostade (eds)
Studies in Late Modern English Correspondence. Methodology and Data.
291 pages. 2008. ISBN 978-3-03911-658-4

Vol. 77 Ingrid Tieken-Boon van Ostade & Wim van der Wurff (eds)
Current Issues in Late Modern English.
436 pages. 2009. ISBN 978-3-03911-660-7

Vol. 78 Marta Navarro Coy (ed.)
Practical Approaches to Foreign Language Teaching and Learning.
297 pages. 2009. ISBN 978-3-03911-661-4

Vol. 79 Qing Ma
Second Language Vocabulary Acquisition.
333 pages. 2009. ISBN 978-3-03911-666-9

Vol. 80 Martin Solly, Michelangelo Conoscenti & Sandra Campagna (eds)
Verbal/Visual Narrative Texts in Higher Education.
384 pages. 2008. ISBN 978-3-03911-672-0

Vol. 81 Meiko Matsumoto
From Simple Verbs to Periphrastic Expressions:
The Historical Development of Composite Predicates, Phrasal Verbs,
and Related Constructions in English.
235 pages. 2008. ISBN 978-3-03911-675-1

Vol. 82 Melinda Dooly
Doing Diversity. Teachers' Construction of Their Classroom Reality.
180 pages. 2009. ISBN 978-3-03911-687-4

Vol. 83 Victoria Guillén-Nieto, Carmen Marimón-Llorca & Chelo Vargas-Sierra (eds)
Intercultural Business Communication and
Simulation and Gaming Methodology.
392 pages. 2009. ISBN 978-3-03911-688-1

Vol. 84 Maria Grazia Guido
English as a Lingua Franca in Cross-cultural Immigration Domains.
285 pages. 2008. ISBN 978-3-03911-689-8

Vol. 85 Erik Castello
Text Complexity and Reading Comprehension Tests.
352 pages. 2008. ISBN 978-3-03911-717-8

Vol. 86 Maria-Lluisa Gea-Valor, Isabel García-Izquierdo & Maria-José Esteve (eds)
Linguistic and Translation Studies in Scientific Communication.
317 pages. 2010. ISBN 978-3-0343-0069-8

Vol. 87 Carmen Navarro, Rosa Mª Rodríguez Abella, Francesca Dalle Pezze
& Renzo Miotti (eds)
La comunicación especializada.
355 pages. 2008. ISBN 978-3-03911-733-8

Vol. 88 Kiriko Sato
The Development from Case-Forms to Prepositional Constructions in Old English Prose.
231 pages. 2009. ISBN 978-3-03911-763-5

Vol. 89 Dorothee Heller (Hrsg.)
Formulierungsmuster in deutscher und italienischer Fachkommunikation. Intra- und interlinguale Perspektiven.
315 pages. 2008. ISBN 978-3-03911-778-9

Vol. 90 Henning Bergenholtz, Sandro Nielsen & Sven Tarp (eds)
Lexicography at a Crossroads. Dictionaries and Encyclopedias Today, Lexicographical Tools Tomorrow.
372 pages. 2009. ISBN 978-3-03911-799-4

Vol. 91 Manouchehr Moshtagh Khorasani
The Development of Controversies. From the Early Modern Period to Online Discussion Forums.
317 pages. 2009. ISBN 978-3-3911-711-6

Vol. 92 María Luisa Carrió-Pastor (ed.)
Content and Language Integrated Learning. Cultural Diversity.
178 pages. 2009. ISBN 978-3-3911-818-2

Vol. 93 Roger Berry
Terminology in English Language Teaching. Nature and Use.
262 pages. 2010. ISBN 978-3-0343-0013-1

Vol. 94 Roberto Cagliero & Jennifer Jenkins (eds)
Discourses, Communities, and Global Englishes
240 pages. 2010. ISBN 978-3-0343-0012-4

Vol. 95 Facchinetti Roberta, Crystal David, Seidlhofer Barbara (eds)
From International to Local English – And Back Again.
268 pages. 2010. ISBN 978-3-0343-0011-7

Vol. 96 Cesare Gagliardi & Alan Maley (eds)
EIL, ELF, Global English. Teaching and Learning Issues
376 pages. 2010. ISBN 978-3-0343-0010-0

Vol. 97 Sylvie Hancil (ed.)
The Role of Prosody in Affective Speech.
403 pages. 2009. ISBN 978-3-03911-696-6

Vol. 98 Marina Dossena & Roger Lass (eds)
Studies in English and European Historical Dialectology.
257 pages. 2009. ISBN 978-3-0343-0024-7

Vol. 99 Christine Béal
Les interactions quotidiennes en français et en anglais. De l'approche comparative à l'analyse des situations interculturelles.
424 pages. 2010. ISBN 978-3-0343-0027-8

Vol. 100 Maurizio Gotti (ed.)
Commonality and Individuality in Academic Discourse.
398 pages. 2009. ISBN 978-3-0343-0023-0

Vol. 101 Javier E. Díaz Vera & Rosario Caballero (eds)
Textual Healing. Studies in Medieval English Medical, Scientific and Technical Texts.
213 pages. 2009. ISBN 978-3-03911-822-9

Vol. 102 Nuria Edo Marzá
The Specialised Lexicographical Approach. A Step further in Dictionary-making.
316 pages. 2009. ISBN 978-3-0343-0043-8

Vol. 103 Carlos Prado-Alonso, Lidia Gómez-García, Iria Pastor-Gómez &
David Tizón-Couto (eds)
New Trends and Methodologies in Applied English Language Research.
Diachronic, Diatopic and Contrastive Studies.
348 pages. 2009. ISBN 978-3-0343-0046-9

Vol. 104 Françoise Salager-Meyer & Beverly A. Lewin
Crossed Words. Criticism in Scholarly Writing?
371 pages. 2011. ISBN 978-3-0343-0049-0.

Vol. 105 Javier Ruano-García
Early Modern Northern English Lexis. A Literary Corpus-Based Study.
611 pages. 2010. ISBN 978-3-0343-0058-2

Vol. 106 Rafael Monroy-Casas
Systems for the Phonetic Transcription of English. Theory and Texts.
280 pages. 2011. ISBN 978-3-0343-0059-9

Vol. 107 Nicola T. Owtram
The Pragmatics of Academic Writing.
A Relevance Approach to the Analysis of Research Article Introductions.
311 pages. 2009. ISBN 978-3-0343-0060-5

Vol. 108 Yolanda Ruiz de Zarobe, Juan Manuel Sierra &
Francisco Gallardo del Puerto (eds)
Content and Foreign Language Integrated Learning.
Contributions to Multilingualism in European Contexts
343 pages. 2011. ISBN 978-3-0343-0074-2

Vol. 109 Ángeles Linde López & Rosalía Crespo Jiménez (eds)
Professional English in the European context. The EHEA challenge.
374 pages. 2010. ISBN 978-3-0343-0088-9

Vol. 110 Rosalía Rodríguez-Vázquez
The Rhythm of Speech, Verse and Vocal Music. A New Theory.
394 pages. 2010. ISBN 978-3-0343-0309-5

Vol. 111 Anastasios Tsangalidis & Roberta Facchinetti (eds)
Studies on English Modality. In Honour of Frank Palmer.
392 pages. 2009. ISBN 978-3-0343-0310-1

Vol. 112 Jing Huang
Autonomy, Agency and Identity in Foreign Language Learning and Teaching.
400 pages. 2013. ISBN 978-3-0343-0370-5

Vol. 113 Mihhail Lotman & Maria-Kristiina Lotman (eds)
Frontiers in Comparative Prosody. In memoriam: Mikhail Gasparov.
426 pages. 2011. ISBN 978-3-0343-0373-6

Vol. 114 Merja Kytö, John Scahill & Harumi Tanabe (eds)
Language Change and Variation from Old English to Late Modern English.
A Festschrift for Minoji Akimoto
422 pages. 2010. ISBN 978-3-0343-0372-9

Vol. 115 Giuliana Garzone & Paola Catenaccio (eds)
Identities across Media and Modes. Discursive Perspectives.
379 pages. 2009. ISBN 978-3-0343-0386-6

Vol. 116 Elena Landone
Los marcadores del discurso y cortesía verbal en español.
390 pages. 2010. ISBN 978-3-0343-0413-9

Vol. 117 Maurizio Gotti & Christopher Williams (eds)
Legal Discourse across Languages and Cultures.
339 pages. 2010. ISBN 978-3-0343-0425-2

Vol. 118 David Hirsh
Academic Vocabulary in Context.
217 pages. 2010. ISBN 978-3-0343-0426-9

Vol. 119 Yvonne Dröschel
Lingua Franca English. The Role of Simplification and Transfer.
358 pages. 2011. ISBN 978-3-0343-0432-0

Vol. 120 Tengku Sepora Tengku Mahadi, Helia Vaezian & Mahmoud Akbari
Corpora in Translation. A Practical Guide.
135 pages. 2010. ISBN 978-3-0343-0434-4

Vol. 121 Davide Simone Giannoni & Celina Frade (eds)
Researching Language and the Law. Textual Features and Translation Issues.
278 pages. 2010. ISBN 978-3-0343-0443-6

Vol. 122 Daniel Madrid & Stephen Hughes (eds)
Studies in Bilingual Education.
472 pages. 2011. ISBN 978-3-0343-0474-0

Vol. 123 Vijay K. Bhatia, Christopher N. Candlin & Maurizio Gotti (eds)
The Discourses of Dispute Resolution.
290 pages. 2010. ISBN 978-3-0343-0476-4

Vol. 124 Davide Simone Giannoni
Mapping Academic Values in the Disciplines. A Corpus-Based Approach.
288 pages. 2010. ISBN 978-3-0343-0488-7

Vol. 125 Giuliana Garzone & James Archibald (eds)
Discourse, Identities and Roles in Specialized Communication.
419 pages. 2010. ISBN 978-3-0343-0494-8

Vol. 126 Iria Pastor-Gómez
The Status and Development of N+N Sequences in
Contemporary English Noun Phrases.
216 pages. 2011. ISBN 978-3-0343-0534-1

Vol. 127 Carlos Prado-Alonso
Full-verb Inversion in Written and Spoken English.
261 pages. 2011. ISBN 978-3-0343-0535-8

Vol. 128 Tony Harris & María Moreno Jaén (eds)
Corpus Linguistics in Language Teaching.
214 pages. 2010. ISBN 978-3-0343-0524-2

Vol. 129 Tetsuji Oda & Hiroyuki Eto (eds)
Multiple Perspectives on English Philology and History of Linguistics.
A Festschrift for Shoichi Watanabe on his 80th Birthday.
378 pages. 2010. ISBN 978-3-0343-0480-1

Vol. 130 Luisa Chierichetti & Giovanni Garofalo (eds)
Lengua y Derecho. líneas de investigación interdisciplinaria.
283 pages. 2010. 978-3-0343-0463-4

Vol. 131 Paola Evangelisti Allori & Giuliana Garzone (eds)
Discourse, Identities and Genres in Corporate Communication.
Sponsorship, Advertising and Organizational Communication.
324 pages. 2011. 978-3-0343-0591-4

Vol. 132 Leyre Ruiz de Zarobe & Yolanda Ruiz de Zarobe (eds)
Speech Acts and Politeness across Languages and Cultures.
402 pages. 2012. 978-3-0343-0611-9

Vol. 133 Thomas Christiansen
Cohesion. A Discourse Perspective.
387 pages. 2011. 978-3-0343-0619-5

Vol. 134 Giuliana Garzone & Maurizio Gotti
Discourse, Communication and the Enterprise. Genres and Trends.
451 pages. 2011. ISBN 978-3-0343-0620-1

Vol. 135 Zsuzsa Hoffmann
Ways of the World's Words.
Language Contact in the Age of Globalization.
334 pages 2011. ISBN 978-3-0343-0673-7

Vol. 136 Cecilia Varcasia (ed.)
Becoming Multilingual.
Language Learning and Language Policy between Attitudes and Identities.
213 pages. 2011. ISBN 978-3-0343-0687-5

Vol. 137 Susy Macqueen
The Emergence of Patterns in Second Language Writing.
A Sociocognitive Exploration of Lexical Trails.
325 pages. 2012. ISBN 978-3-0343-1010-9

Vol. 138 Maria Vittoria Calvi & Giovanna Mapelli (eds)
La lengua del turismo. Géneros discursivos y terminología.
365 pages. 2011. ISBN 978-3-0343-1011-6

Vol. 139 Ken Lau
Learning to Become a Professional in a Textually-Mediated World.
A Text-Oriented Study of Placement Practices.
261 pages. 2012. ISBN 978-3-0343-1016-1

Vol. 140 Sandra Campagna, Giuliana Garzone, Cornelia Ilie & Elizabeth Rowley-Jolivet (eds)
Evolving Genres in Web-mediated Communication.
337 pages. 2012. ISBN 978-3-0343-1013-0

Vol. 141 Edith Esch & Martin Solly (eds)
The Sociolinguistics of Language Education in International Contexts.
263 pages. 2012. ISBN 978-3-0343-1009-3

Vol. 142 Forthcoming.

Vol. 143 David Tizón-Couto
Left Dislocation in English. A Functional-Discoursal Approach.
416 pages. 2012. ISBN 978-3-0343-1037-6

Vol. 144 Margrethe Petersen & Jan Engberg (eds)
Current Trends in LSP Research. Aims and Methods.
323 pages. 2011. ISBN 978-3-0343-1054-3

Vol. 145 David Tizón-Couto, Beatriz Tizón-Couto, Iria Pastor-Gómez & Paula Rodríguez-Puente (eds)
New Trends and Methodologies in Applied English Language Research II.
Studies in Language Variation, Meaning and Learning.
283 pages. 2012. ISBN 978-3-0343-1061-1

Vol. 146 Rita Salvi & Hiromasa Tanaka (eds)
Intercultural Interactions in Business and Management.
306 pages. 2011. ISBN 978-3-0343-1039-0

Vol. 147 Francesco Straniero Sergio & Caterina Falbo (eds)
Breaking Ground in Corpus-based Interpreting Studies.
254 pages. 2012. ISBN 978-3-0343-1071-0

Vol. 148 Forthcoming.

Vol. 149 Vijay K. Bhatia & Paola Evangelisti Allori (eds)
Discourse and Identity in the Professions. Legal, Corporate and Institutional Citizenship.
352 pages. 2011. ISBN 978-3-0343-1079-6

Vol. 150 Maurizio Gotti (ed.)
Academic Identity Traits. A Corpus-Based Investigation.
363 pages. 2012. ISBN 978-3-0343-1141-0

Vol. 151 Priscilla Heynderickx, Sylvain Dieltjens, Geert Jacobs, Paul Gillaerts &
Elizabeth de Groot (eds)
The Language Factor in International Business.
New Perspectives on Research, Teaching and Practice.
320 pages. 2012. ISBN 978-3-0343-1090-1

Vol. 152 Paul Gillaerts, Elizabeth de Groot, Sylvain Dieltjens, Priscilla Heynderickx &
Geert Jacobs (eds)
Researching Discourse in Business Genres. Cases and Corpora.
215 pages. 2012. ISBN 978-3-0343-1092-5

Vol. 153 Yongyan Zheng
Dynamic Vocabulary Development in a Foreign Language.
262 pages. 2012. ISBN 978-3-0343-1106-9

Vol. 154 Carmen Argondizzo (ed.)
Creativity and Innovation in Language Education.
357 pages. 2012. ISBN 978-3-0343-1080-2

Vol. 155 David Hirsh (ed.)
Current Perspectives in Second Language Vocabulary Research.
180 pages. 2012. ISBN 978-3-0343-1108-3

Vol. 156 Seiji Shinkawa
Unhistorical Gender Assignment in Lahamon's *Brut*. A Case Study of a Late Stage
in the Development of Grammatical Gender toward its Ultimate Loss.
186 pages. 2012. ISBN 978-3-0343-1124-3

Vol. 157 Yeonkwon Jung
Basics of Organizational Writing: A Critical Reading Approach.
151 pages. 2014. ISBN 978-3-0343-1137-3.

Vol. 158 Bárbara Eizaga Rebollar (ed.)
Studies in Linguistics and Cognition.
301 pages. 2012. ISBN 978-3-0343-1138-0

Vol. 159 Giuliana Garzone, Paola Catenaccio, Chiara Degano (eds)
Genre Change in the Contemporary World. Short-term Diachronic Perspectives.
329 pages. 2012. ISBN 978-3-0343-1214-1

Vol. 160 Carol Berkenkotter, Vijay K. Bhatia & Maurizio Gotti (eds)
Insights into Academic Genres.
468 pages. 2012. ISBN 978-3-0343-1211-0

Vol. 161 Beatriz Tizón-Couto
Clausal Complements in Native and Learner Spoken English. A corpus-based study with Lindsei and Vicolse. 357 pages. 2013. ISBN 978-3-0343-1184-7

Vol. 162 Patrizia Anesa
Jury Trials and the Popularization of Legal Language. A Discourse Analytical Approach.
247 pages. 2012. ISBN 978-3-0343-1231-8

Vol. 163 David Hirsh
Endangered Languages, Knowledge Systems and Belief Systems.
153 pages. 2013. ISBN 978-3-0343-1232-5

Vol. 164 Eugenia Sainz (ed.)
De la estructura de la frase al tejido del discurso. Estudios contrastivos español/italiano.
305 pages. 2014. ISBN 978-3-0343-1253-0

Vol. 165 Julia Bamford, Franca Poppi & Davide Mazzi (eds)
Space, Place and the Discursive Construction of Identity.
367 pages. 2014. ISBN 978-3-0343-1249-3

Vol. 166 Rita Salvi & Janet Bowker (eds)
Space, Time and the Construction of Identity.
Discursive Indexicality in Cultural, Institutional and Professional Fields.
324 pages. 2013. ISBN 978-3-0343-1254-7

Vol. 167 Shunji Yamazaki & Robert Sigley (eds)
Approaching Language Variation through Corpora. A Festschrift in Honour of Toshio Saito.
421 pages. 2013. ISBN 978-3-0343-1264-6

Vol. 168 Franca Poppi
Global Interactions in English as a Lingua Franca. How written communication is changing under the influence of electronic media and new contexts of use.
249 pages. 2012. ISBN 978-3-0343-1276-9

Vol. 169 Miguel A. Aijón Oliva & María José Serrano
Style in syntax. Investigating variation in Spanish pronoun subjects.
239 pages. 2013. ISBN 978-3-0343-1244-8

Vol. 170 Inés Olza, Óscar Loureda & Manuel Casado-Velarde (eds)
Language Use in the Public Sphere. Methodological Perspectives and Empirical Applications
564 pages. 2014. ISBN 978-3-0343-1286-8

Vol. 171 Aleksandra Matulewska
Legilinguistic Translatology. A Parametric Approach to Legal Translation.
279 pages. 2013. ISBN 978-3-0343-1287-5

Vol. 172 Maurizio Gotti & Carmen Sancho Guinda (eds)
Narratives in Academic and Professional Genres.
513 pages. 2013. ISBN 978-3-0343-1371-1

Vol. 173 Madalina Chitez
Learner corpus profiles. The case of Romanian Learner English.
244 pages. 2014. ISBN 978-3-0343-1410-7

Vol. 174 Chihiro Inoue
Task Equivalence in Speaking Tests.
251 pages. 2013. ISBN 978-3-0343-1417-6

Vol. 175 Gabriel Quiroz & Pedro Patiño (eds.)
LSP in Colombia: advances and challenges.
339 pages. 2014. ISBN 978-3-0343-1434-3

Vol. 176 Catherine Resche
Economic Terms and Beyond: Capitalising on the Wealth of Notions.
How Researchers in Specialised Varieties of English Can Benefit from Focusing on Terms.
332 pages. 2013. ISBN 978-3-0343-1435-0

Vol. 177 Wei Wang
Media Representation of Migrant Workers in China. Identities and Stances.
198 pages. 2017. ISBN 978-3-0343-1436-7

Vol. 178 Cécile Desoutter & Caroline Mellet (dir.)
Le discours rapporté: approches linguistiques et perspectives didactiques.
270 pages. 2013. ISBN 978-3-0343-1292-9

Vol. 179 Ana Díaz-Negrillo & Francisco Javier Díaz-Pérez (eds)
Specialisation and Variation in Language Corpora.
341 pages. 2014. ISBN 978-3-0343-1316-2

Vol. 180 Pilar Alonso
A Multi-dimensional Approach to Discourse Coherence. From Standardness to Creativity.
247 pages. 2014. ISBN 978-3-0343-1325-4

Vol. 181 Alejandro Alcaraz-Sintes & Salvador Valera-Hernández (eds)
Diachrony and Synchrony in English Corpus Linguistics.
393 pages. 2014. ISBN 978-3-0343-1326-1

Vol. 182 Runhan Zhang
Investigating Linguistic Knowledge of a Second Language.
207 pages. 2015. ISBN 978-3-0343-1330-8

Vol. 183 Hajar Abdul Rahim & Shakila Abdul Manan (eds.)
English in Malaysia. Postcolonial and Beyond.
267 pages. 2014. ISBN 978-3-0343-1341-4

Vol. 184 Virginie Fasel Lauzon
Comprendre et apprendre dans l'interaction. Les séquences d'explication en classe de français langue seconde.
292 pages. 2014. ISBN 978-3-0343-1451-0

Vol. 185 Forthcoming.

Vol. 186 Wei Ren
L2 Pragmatic Development in Study Abroad Contexts
256 pages. 2015. ISBN 978-3-0343-1358-2

Vol. 187 Marina Bondi & Rosa Lorés Sanz (eds)
Abstracts in Academic Discourse. Variation and Change.
361 pages. 2014. ISBN 978-3-0343-1483-1

Vol. 188 Forthcoming.

Vol. 189 Paola Evangelisti Allori (ed.)
Identities in and across Cultures.
315 pages. 2014. ISBN 978-3-0343-1458-9

Vol. 190 Erik Castello, Katherine Ackerley & Francesca Coccetta (eds).
Studies in Learner Corpus Linguistics. Research and Applications for Foreign Language Teaching and Assessment.
358 pages. 2015. ISBN 978-3-0343-1506-7

Vol. 191 Ruth Breeze, Maurizio Gotti & Carmen Sancho Guinda (eds)
Interpersonality in Legal Genres.
389 pages. 2014. ISBN 978-3-0343-1524-1

Vol. 192 Paola Evangelisti Allori, John Bateman & Vijay K. Bhatia (eds)
Evolution in Genre. Emergence, Variation, Multimodality.
364 pages. 2014. ISBN 978-3-0343-1533-3

Vol. 193 Jiyeon Kook
Agency in Arzt-Patient-Gesprächen. Zur interaktionistischen Konzeptualisierung von Agency
271 pages. 2015. ISBN 978-3-0343-1666-8

Vol. 194 Susana Nicolás Román & Juan José Torres Núñez (eds)
Drama and CLIL. A new challenge for the teaching approaches in bilingual education.
170 pages. 2015. ISBN 978-3-0343-1629-3

Vol. 195 Alessandra Molino & Serenella Zanotti (eds)
Observing Norm, Observing Usage. Lexis in Dictionaries and in the Media.
430 pages. 2015. ISBN 978-3-0343-1584-5

Vol. 196 Begoña Soneira
A Lexical Description of English for Architecture. A Corpus-based Approach.
267 pages. 2015. ISBN 978-3-0343-1602-6

Vol. 197 M Luisa Roca-Varela
False Friends in Learner Corpora. A corpus-based study of English false friends in the written and spoken production of Spanish learners.
348 pages. 2015. ISBN 978-3-0343-1620-0

Vol. 198 Rahma Al-Mahrooqi & Christopher Denman
Bridging the Gap between Education and Employment. English Language Instruction in EFL Contexts.
416 pages. 2015. ISBN 978-3-0343-1681-1

Vol. 199 Rita Salvi & Janet Bowker (eds)
The Dissemination of Contemporary Knowledge in English. Genres, discourse strategies and professional practices.
171 pages. 2015. ISBN 978-3-0343-1679-8

Vol. 200 Maurizio Gotti & Davide S. Giannoni (eds)
Corpus Analysis for Descriptive and Pedagogical Purposes. ESP Perspectives.
432 pages. 2014. ISBN 978-3-0343-1516-6

Vol. 201 Ida Ruffolo
The Perception of Nature in Travel Promotion Texts. A Corpus-based Discourse Analysis.
148 pages. 2015. ISBN 978-3-0343-1521-0

Vol. 202 Ives Trevian
English suffixes. Stress-assignment properties, productivity, selection and combinatorial processes.
471 pages. 2015. ISBN 978-3-0343-1576-0

Vol. 203 Maurizio Gotti, Stefania Maci & Michele Sala (eds)
Insights into Medical Communication.
422 pages. 2015. ISBN 978-3-0343-1694-1

Vol. 204 Carmen Argondizzo (ed.)
European Projects in University Language Centres. Creativity, Dynamics, Best Practice.
371 pages. 2015. ISBN 978-3-0343-1696-5

Vol. 205 Aura Luz Duffé Montalván (ed.)
Estudios sobre el léxico. Puntos y contrapuntos.
502 pages. 2016. ISBN 978-3-0343-2011-5

Vol. 206 Maria Pavesi, Maicol Formentelli & Elisa Ghia (eds)
The Languages of Dubbing. Mainstream Audiovisual Translation in Italy.
275 pages. 2014. ISBN 978-3-0343-1646-0

Vol. 207 Ruth Breeze & Inés Olza (eds)
Evaluation in media discourse. European perspectives.
268 pages. 2017. ISBN 978-3-0343-2014-6

Vol. 208 Vijay K. Bhatia & Maurizio Gotti (eds)
Arbitration Discourse in Asia.
331 pages. 2015. ISBN 978-3-0343-2032-0

Vol. 209 Sofía Bemposta-Rivas, Carla Bouzada-Jabois, Yolanda Fernández-Pena, Tamara Bouso, Yolanda J. Calvo-Benzies, Iván Tamaredo (eds)
New trends and methodologies in applied English language research III. Synchronic and diachronic studies on discourse, lexis and grammar processing.
280 pages. 2017. ISBN 978-3-0343-2039-9

Vol. 210 Francisco Alonso Almeida, Laura Cruz García & Víctor González Ruiz (eds)
Corpus-based studies on language varieties.
285 pages. 2016. ISBN 978-3-0343-2044-3

Vol. 211 Juan Pedro Rica Peromingo
Aspectos lingüísticos y técnicos de la traducción audiovisual (TAV).
177 pages. 2016. ISBN 978-3-0343-2055-9

Vol. 212 Maria Vender
Disentangling Dyslexia. VenderPhonological and Processing Deficit in Developmental Dyslexia.
338 pages. 2017. ISBN 978-3-0343-2064-1

Vol. 213 Zhilong Xie
Bilingual Advantages. Contributions of Different Bilingual Experiences to Cognitive Control Differences Among Young-adult Bilinguals.
221 pages. 2016. ISBN 978-3-0343-2081-8

Vol. 214 Larissa D'Angelo
Academic posters. A textual and visual metadiscourse analysis.
367 pages. 2016. ISBN 978-3-0343-2083-2

Vol. 215 Evelyne Berger
Prendre la parole en L2. Regard sur la compétence d'interaction en classe de langue.
246 pages. 2016. ISBN 978-3-0343-2084-9

Vol. 216 David Lasagabaster and Aintzane Doiz (eds)
CLIL experiences in secondary and tertiary education: In search of good practices.
262 pages. 2016. ISBN 978-3-0343-2104-4

Vol. 217 Elena Kkese
Identifying Plosives in L2 English: The Case of L1 Cypriot Greek Speakers.
317 pages. 2016. ISBN 978-3-0343-2060-3

Vol. 218 Sandra Campagna, Elana Ochse, Virginia Pulcini & Martin Solly (eds)
Languaging in and across Communities: New Voices, New Identities. Studies in Honour of Giuseppina Cortese.
507 pages. 2016. ISBN 978-3-0343-2073-3

Vol. 219 Adriana Orlandi & Laura Giacomini (ed.)
Defining collocation for lexicographic purposes. From linguistic theory to lexicographic practice.
328 pages. 2016. ISBN 978-3-0343-2054-2

Vol. 220 Pietro Luigi Iaia
Analysing English as a Lingua Franca in Video Games. Linguistic Features, Experiential and Functional Dimensions of Online and Scripted Interactions.
139 pages. 2016. ISBN 978-3-0343-2138-9

Vol. 221 Dimitrinka G. Níkleva (ed.)
La formación de los docentes de español para inmigrantes en distintos contextos educativos.
390 pages. 2017. ISBN 978-3-0343-2135-8

Vol. 222 Katherine Ackerley, Marta Guarda & Francesca Helm (eds)
Sharing Perspectives on English-Medium Instruction.
308 pages. 2017. ISBN 978-3-0343-2537-0

Vol. 223 Juana I. Marín-Arrese, Julia Lavid-López, Marta Carretero, Elena Domínguez Romero, Mª Victoria Martín de la Rosa & María Pérez Blanco (eds)
Evidentiality and Modality in European Languages. Discourse-pragmatic perspectives.
427 pages. 2017. ISBN 978-3-0343-2437-3

Vol. 224 Gilles Col
Construction du sens : un modèle instructionnel pour la sémantique.
292 pages. 2017. ISBN 978-3-0343-2572-1

Vol. 225 Ana Chiquito & Gabriel Quiroz (eds)
Pobreza, Lenguaje y Medios en América Latina.
362 pages. 2017. ISBN 978-3-0343-2142-6

Vol. 226 Xu Zhang
English Quasi-Numeral Classifiers. A Corpus-Based Cognitive-Typological Study.
360 pages. 2017. ISBN 978-3-0343-2818-0

Vol. 227 María Ángeles Orts, Ruth Breeze & Maurizio Gotti (eds)
Power, Persuasion and Manipulation in Specialised Genres. Providing Keys to the Rhetoric of Professional Communities.
368 pages. 2017. ISBN 978-3-0343-3010-7

Vol. 228 Maurizio Gotti, Stefania Maci & Michele Sala (eds)
Ways of Seeing, Ways of Being: Representing the Voices of Tourism.
453 pages. 2017. ISBN 978-3-0343-3031-2

Vol. 229 Forthcoming.

Vol. 230 Anca-Cristina Sterie
Interprofessional interactions at the hospital. Nurses' requests and reports of problems in calls with physicians.
371 pages. 2017. ISBN 978-3-0343-2734-3

Vol. 231 Xiaodong Zhang
Understanding Chinese EFL Teachers' Beliefs and Practices in the Textbook-Based Classroom.
189 pages. 2017. ISBN 978-3-0343-3053-4

Vol. 232 Manuela Caterina Moroni & Federica Ricci Garotti (Hrsg.)
Brücken schlagen zwischen Sprachwissenschaft und DaF-Didaktik.
345 pages. 2017. ISBN 978-3-0343-2667-4

www.ingramcontent.com/pod-product-compliance
Ingram Content Group UK Ltd.
Pitfield, Milton Keynes, MK11 3LW, UK
UKHW020718041026
15590UKWH00002B/750

9 783034 314367